LB 2343 S48 Shaffer, R.
Student personnel services in higher education

Student Personnel Services in Higher Education

THE LIBRARY OF EDUCATION

A Project of The Center for Applied Research in Education, Inc.

G. R. Gottschalk, Director

Categories of Coverage

I	II	III
Curriculum and Teaching	Administration, Organization, and Finance	Psychology for Educators
IV	**V**	**VI**
History, Philosophy, and Social Foundations	Professional Skills	Educational Institutions

Student Personnel Services in Higher Education

ROBERT H. SHAFFER

Dean of Students and Professor of Education
Indiana University

WILLIAM D. MARTINSON

Assistant Dean of Students, Director of Counseling
and Professor of Education, Indiana University

The Center for Applied Research in Education, Inc.
New York

LIBRARY OF CONGRESS
CATALOG CARD NO.: 66-19211

PRINTED IN THE UNITED STATES OF AMERICA

Foreword

Concern for the moral, spiritual, and physical welfare of students has been an integral part of American higher education since the founding of Harvard College in 1636. From colonial days to the latter part of the Nineteenth Century, this concern was expressed primarily through the college president and his faculty, many of whom were clergymen. Between the years 1870 and 1930, a thirty-fold expansion of student population took place making it necessary for colleges to delegate the responsibility for extra-class student affairs to specific staff members. The president and other administrators became more and more preoccupied with the tasks of securing money, recruiting staff, erecting buildings, revising the curriculum, engaging in public service, and developing long range plans. Faculty members became more and more preoccupied with the increasing demands of teaching, research, publication, and public service. Only by assigning the neglected tasks to specialists such as deans of women, deans of men, and residence hall supervisors was a breakdown of institutional concern for extra-class life averted.

As the industrial and educational world became more and more complex, students were faced with the problem of making choices for which they had insufficient background, inadequate information, and practically no experience. They became bruised and shocked by many factors when trying to realize the "American dream" of acquiring a college degree. Some found that their level of academic achievement was inadequate; that social distractions and conflicting "values" hampered learning; that competition for openings to graduate or professional schools was extremely keen; that sufficient funds to stay in college were lacking. As a result, colleges were forced to assist students in meeting these pressures and related problems by providing such services as housing, counseling, supervision of social behavior, student employment as well as health services. What is now thought of as the student personnel program of a college or university is actually a group of formally structured services and offices which grew up in response to the needs of the collegiate community.

If institutions of higher education had not met the needs of their supporting society, as represented by what are often termed pressure groups, higher education would not have had popular support for expansion. If they had failed to meet the needs of the unsophisticated or disadvantaged college-age youth, the growth of the country would have been stunted from each of needed leadership and skilled personnel. Without the broad base of trained manpower provided by colleges and universities, the United States would not have been able to develop as rapidly and with such diversity as it has during the Twentieth Century.

Currently, higher education in the United States is faced with demands similar to those which it has met successfully in the past. The confusing multiplicity of demands both for special educational programs and for extended public service indicates how great the need is today for colleges and universities to meet the challenge anew—with imagination, creativity, flexibility, and resilience. Young people cannot be educated for change within set patterns and rigid procedures. Neither can educators "educate for change" if they are not willing to change.

Just as American colleges and universities responded to past challenges resourcefully and effectively, so they must meet the demands of today's turbulent world. Student personnel work represents a significant factor in contributing toward that end.

HERMAN B WELLS
Chancellor, Indiana University

Student Personnel Services in Higher Education

Shaffer and Martinson

For purposes of analysis higher education may divide its operational functions into four major areas: academic affairs, student affairs, business and financial affairs, and public relations. Shaffer and Martinson treat the second of these areas in this book. Within an institution of higher education administrative responsibilities toward student affairs is generally known as student personnel services. Broadly defined, student personnel service includes all the institution's relations with the students except those of actual classroom instruction.

Both authors are professors of education at Indiana University, and both hold positions of major responsibility in the student personnel services there. Dr. Shaffer is Dean of Students and is in general charge of the student personnel services; Dr. Martinson is Assistant Dean of Students and Director of Counseling. Both are men of broad experience in the field.

In their book the authors' concern is focused almost exclusively on the student and his education. Their basic premise is that student personnel services exist for the purpose of furthering the education of students—using a broad interpretation of the term "education." Their approach is positive, and their writing is centered around ways in which institutional resources and student energies may be directed so that the greatest possible educational gains result. They reject the negative approach which would look upon student personnel services, from the older disciplinary point of view, as a device for repressing and restricting students' activities and conduct—in the belief that this induces the students to devote more time to study.

The book covers a wide field, with chapters devoted to topics such as recruitment and orientation, financial aid, counseling, health services, student housing, and student extra-class activities. Significantly there is no whole chapter devoted to student discipline, though the subject comes up several times within the book. The authors discuss frankly and objectively the thorny problem of "student freedom," currently a "hot issue" on many college and university campuses in the United States. In a book covering such a broad field, no one topic can be treated exhaustively. A well-selected bibliography at the end of the volume suggests further readings.

Student Personnel Services in Higher Education complements certain other volumes in the Library of Education. This book parallels treatment of the same topic at the elementary and secondary school level in *Pupil Personnel Services* by Donald G. Ferguson. *Student Activities in American Education* by Robert W. Frederick treats the subject on all levels of education, giving considerable emphasis to the secondary school.

JOHN DALE RUSSELL
Content Editor

Contents

CHAPTER VI

CHAPTER VII

CHAPTER VIII

CHAPTER I

Philosophy and Objectives of Student Personnel Services

The generalized goal of education in America is developing the individual to such a degree that he is best equipped to assume his complex role as a citizen in an industrialized, technologically oriented, socially oriented, democratic society. In both publicly and privately controlled institutions of higher education the goals are generally those of preserving, transmitting, and enriching the body of knowledge which is the heritage of successive generations. More than that, higher education strives to develop leaders who will take their place in a democratic society—dedicated to the preservation and advancement of the values prized by the society which raised and nurtured them. Thus, education is concerned both with knowledge and with individuals: placing high priority upon the depth and breadth of knowledge to be attained and at the same time striving to develop individuals.

These are the goals of higher education and within the institutions themselves it is the primary goal of student personnel service to assist each person admitted to fully develop his potential through the effective and efficient use of the resources of that institution.

Essentially, emphasis both in modern higher education and in modern student personnel work is upon developing responsibility in the individual for his own growth and development. A college or university is basically a collection of resources available to students. One function of the student personnel worker is to motivate, stimulate, and enable the student to make effective use of these resources. The student who profits most from his university experience is the one who takes advantage of the many opportunities to learn new ideas, learns to weigh and consider facts, discusses and debates issues, and utilizes his personal skills. These opportunities may occur outside of the classroom or within it. Student personnel service, therefore, being concerned with the whole student in his total environment, recognizes that what the student learns and experiences in his out-of-class life has a direct bearing upon his aspirations, motives, and achievements in class.

Student personnel service is based upon the perception that the student's role is that of a responsible, self-directing young adult striving for self-improvement and personal development through higher education.

The Student Personnel Point of View

The essential nature of student personnel work in higher education has been succinctly stated by the Committee on College Personnel of the American Council on Education in a statement entitled "The Student Personnel Point of View."

> The student personnel point of view encompasses the student as a whole. The concept of education is broadened to include attention to the student's well-rounded development—physically, socially, emotionally, and spiritually, as well as intellectually. The student is thought of as a responsible participant in his own development and not as a passive recipient of an imprinted economic, political, or religious doctrine, or vocational skill. As a responsible participant in the societal process of our American democracy, his full and balanced maturity is viewed as a major end-goal of education, and, as well, a necessary means to the fullest development of his fellow citizens. From the personnel point of view any lesser goal falls short of the desired objective and is a real drain and strain upon the self-realization of other developing individuals in our society.
>
> The realization of this objective—the full maturing of each student—cannot be attained without interest in and integrated efforts toward the development of each and every facet of his personality and potentialities.[1]

The student personnel point of view considers each student an individual with a unique constellation of traits to be treated as an indivisible personality functioning and reacting to his environment as a whole. Furthermore, the individual's unique personal make-up is considered a significant factor in his own education and development.

---

[1] *The Student Personnel Point of View,* Council Studies, Series VI, No. 13 (Washington, D.C.: American Council on Education, 1949), p. 1.

Review of the Development of Student Personnel Service in Colleges and Universities

Student personnel service as an organized field has been, until very recently, a unique feature of American higher education. The growth of student personnel services in foreign institutions has been largely the result of exported concepts since World War II. Contrary to some critics, student personnel service did not start for the propagandizing of professionally trained people in the field. Rather, it had its roots in the concern John Harvard and his successors had for the spiritual welfare of students in the early colleges and universities. Historically, higher education was, for the most part, privately controlled and had a strong religious emphasis. Early institutions were characterized as much for their required chapel exercises, church services, and prayer meetings as for their Latin and Greek classes. From 1636 until the Morrill Act of 1862 and the subsequent Land Grant movement, presidents and faculty members engaged in an exaggerated type of student personnel service, concerned primarily with students' pious behavior and their diligent attention to studies.

Part of this concern arose because students formerly entered college at much younger ages than at present; for example, early at Harvard the students were mostly 14 to 17 years of age. Most of the concern, however, came from a conscious social policy in the early colonies, which emphasized the importance of educating all citizens, but particularly males. The Bible was read as a guide to their living, and the Constitution, laws, and other documents governing them as a guide to their participation in a democratic self-government.

In the latter part of the Nineteenth Century and in the early part of the Twentieth a number of developments demanded new procedures and techniques for dealing effectively with large numbers of heterogeneous college students. Along with an explosive increase in college enrollment came an abrupt secularization of education brought about by the broadened view of privately controlled colleges and by the establishment of Land Grant Colleges after the Morrill Act was passed in 1862. In addition, general reaction arose against the objective intellectualism of German-oriented educators and researchers. From the same educators came another new outlook—the application of psychological principles to individual growth and development. All this began in the Twentieth Century and led to the tremendous growth in the personnel movement after World War I.

Coeducation, which started at Oberlin College in 1837, grew into its own in the latter part of the Nineteenth Century, coinciding with the general growth of education. Concern for the physical and moral welfare of women students brought about the employment of matrons, lady principals, and subsequently, deans of women. Almost simultaneous with the rapid growth of student bodies and the introduction of coeducation was the expansion of curricular offerings. The typical pattern of classical studies broadened to include courses necessary to equip citizens to live and work in a rapidly developing, industrial society.

All these forces resulted in a Twentieth Century development now called the student personnel movement. From rather narrow and perfunctory beginnings it has grown into a large, important, and expanding young profession with future limitations not yet in sight.

Essential Elements of a Student Personnel Program

The administrative structure of any enterprise varies greatly with local situations, emphases being placed upon certain functions and values, institutional traditions, personalities, and the degree of formalism present in the sponsoring institution. Any consideration of the most desirable organizational structure for administering student personnel services depends upon the needs of the institution and its dominant characteristics.

Specific student personnel services necessary for a reasonably complete student personnel program have been listed as follows:

1. A program of pre-college counseling, selection, and applicant-centered admissions policies.
2. An organized program for diagnosis of needs and counseling of students. This includes both intensive and clinical counseling, as well as the normal day-to-day educational and personal counseling provided by the faculty and other less technically trained counselors.
3. A continuous orientation program based upon principles and procedures of effective communication.

4. Remedial assistance in reading, speech, English, and other subject-matter areas for those students who need such help.

5. Specific provision for the supervision, coordination, and integration of the out-of-class or co-curricular program on the campus.

6. A student health service, providing professional guidance for both physical well-being and mental health.

7. An adequate program for the supervision of living arrangements, including the food service program. This program, like the others, must contribute, to the greatest extent possible, to the socio-educational objectives of the institution.

8. A well-organized program for administering financial aids such as loans, scholarships, fee discounts, employment, post graduate placement, and employment follow-ups.

9. Special facilities for developing and evaluating the religious life and interests of students on the campus.

10. An adequate system of permanent cumulative personnel records, including pertinent information relative to *all* aspects of the student's life and accomplishments.

11. On many campuses, there is a need for a special program of orientation and counseling for foreign students.[2]

A listing of the services which make up a typical college student personnel program does not necessarily imply that there is a need for separate and specialized offices to render *each* service. Rather, the listing serves to point out functions which need attention on any campus. Frequently, various personnel functions are performed by faculty members whose primary responsibility is teaching. Just as frequently, various functions are combined and performed in a central office. Hence, the student personnel administrator on a campus must marshal resources, organize them into an administrative structure, and supervise all efforts to help the college achieve its goals.

Objectives of Student Personnel Work on the College Campus

From the point of view outlined above, there are several specific objectives which a student personnel program should strive to achieve on any college campus, whether or not various services are

[2] Adapted with minor changes for updating from E. H. Hopkins, "The Essentials of a Student Personnel Program," an address given at the opening session of the annual convention of the American College Personnel Association, March 29, 1948, Chicago, Illinois, *Educational and Psychological Measurement,* 8, No. 3 (1948), pp. 431–432.

organized and classified into a formal program. These may be listed as follows:

1. *To assist in providing a campus climate in student residences and campus affairs which is conducive to academic achievement while providing maximum intellectual stimulation.* This includes the provision of wholesome social and recreational activities which are compatible with the educational environment. Such coherence within the campus climate must arise from the integration of the goals and efforts of students and faculty alike. All elements of the college community contribute to student growth. What the student learns in his out-of-class life determines, to a great extent, the attitudes, the aspirations, and the motivation he brings to the classroom and the level of achievement he attains there.

All staff members of a college must be interested in this environmental influence, not merely the student personnel workers. General agreement on the goals and objectives by all segments of a college and the aggressive realignment of all educational forces within the campus community are essential to a vital and effective academic effort. To be successful in assisting his institution in establishing a sound academic and intellectually oriented environment, the student personnel worker must direct his interests and efforts toward organizing, uniting, and cooperating with all other elements in the college community.

2. *To provide those services which will assist in the self-development of each student and promote the understanding of his own purposes for being in college.* The best interests of any educational enterprise demand that all associated with it clearly understand its general objectives as well as those of specific offices and departments. Students particularly need to understand what the college considers a good education, what it feels marks its greatness and success, and what it expects of its graduates. Just as a definite relationship exists between communication and employee productivity in a business enterprise, so also is there one between the effectiveness of the communication of the spirit and meaning of the college and the productivity of its students.

Many students have goals other than those upon which the college places primary importance. Such students are content with the relative satisfaction of their goals and usually feel little disturbance if they do not live up to the expectancies of the college. This is particularly true when the expectancies of the college are vague and poorly communicated. Because they are satisfied when their own goals are partially attained, some students sincerely do not understand and are not greatly moved by the anguished cries of faculty members and the statements of educational critics that American colleges are not doing an adequate job.

Every institution should examine carefully what it is doing in order to interpret its nature, goals, and expectancies more effectively to its students. Such an examination should include a critical analysis of the literature sent to prospective students, the orientation procedures, the approach and content of opening day classes, the public relation programs, alumni programs, campus extra-curricular programs, and, particularly, the dominant forces in student culture.

The importance of student culture on a campus as an educational force has been emphasized by the reports on the studies at Vassar:

> The student body as an entity may be thought to possess characteristic qualities of personality, ways of interacting socially, types of values and beliefs, and the like, which are passed on from one "generation" of students to another and which like any culture provide a basic context in which individual learning takes place. We contend, in fact, that this culture is the prime educational force at work in the College, for, as we shall see, assimilation into the student society is the foremost concern of most students. Suffice it to say now that, in our opinion, the scholastic and academic aims and processes of the College are, in large measure, transmitted to incoming students or mediated for them by the predominant students' culture.[3]

Thus, any consideration of securing a more coherent campus environment and interpreting the meaning and a significance of this environment to students must take into account the values, the status figures, and forces prevalent in the campus culture.

3. *To provide through student government and other activities an opportunity to practice democratic living with both its rights and responsibilities and to learn to work effectively with others.* What the student experiences determines, to a major extent, his values, his attitudes, and his perceptions of the world. Writings of the last few years highlight an urgent need to attend to the relationship, or the lack of it, between the formation of certain values and a college

---

[3] Mervin B. Freedman, "The Passage Through College," *The Journal of Social Issues,* XII, No. 4 (1956), 14.

education. If colleges are to have serious, motivated, and thinking students on their campuses, they must help their students see their college experience as more than a passage of time. An education must be seen as more than an accumulation of credit hours, or merely as training to earn a better living.

Nevitt Sanford, also reporting on the Vassar research, concluded that students "perceive the curriculum as more or less irrelevant and look to each other for the instruction that really matters."[4] His observations and those of "like-thinkers" may be accurate or not; it, nevertheless, remains that students must find real meaning in their college experiences. It is up to the personnel program to provide agencies and to organize resources to carry out this important function.

An effective program of student government is basic to meaningful and relevant education and must provide a vehicle which encourages and facilitates students' involvement in the day to day decisions of their college or university.

4. *To provide the opportunity for faculty-student contacts outside the classroom as a means of encouraging respect for learning and an understanding of the approach to life's problems.* The relationship of the teacher and student is enhanced when the student has a clear understanding of his professor as a person, scholar, and teacher, as opposed to the all-too-common view of the professor as an enemy, grade-giver, or an intellectual dust-pot.

Out-of-class association provides opportunities for the student to explore questions about the university, its curriculum and courses; to relate classroom experiences with community life; and to form habits of continuous self-directed learning and intellectual exploration which will remain with him all his life. Furthermore, it is through such associations that faculty members secure valuable feedback regarding their own teaching, the teaching of their colleagues, and the impact the institution as a whole has made. Faculty members who do not have any out-of-class association with their students are likely to be sterile in their teaching, boring in their classroom methodology, and ineffective in inspiring their students. Lastly, out-of-class association provides an opportunity

---

[4] Nevitt Sanford, "Changing Sex Roles, Socialization, and Education," *Human Development Bulletin on the Ninth Annual Symposium* (Chicago, Ill.: University of Chicago Press, 1958), p. 66.

for the most effective type of counseling; namely, it provides a situation in which an experienced personal acquaintance in the academic community can interact with the young student who is facing a myriad of complex questions arising from his university experience.

5. *To provide an opportunity for every worthy student to complete his education—providing financial assistance, when necessary, in the form of scholarships, loans, and employment.* The growth of financial aids to college students has been one of the most sensational developments in education since World War II. Beginning with the remarkably successful "G.I. Bill" for veterans, the concept of providing financial aid to students has grown to such a point that the largest institutions operate a multi-million dollar program.

Even small institutions have rapidly expanding programs. The traditional concept of financial aid as being a scholarship, loan, or a job is being replaced with broadly conceived financial "package" consisting of combinations of all types of aid.

The growth of financial aids has exceeded the growth and the cost of attending college but not by a marked degree. Present indications are that the cost of college attendance for future generations will be markedly higher than current rates. In view of the fact that it is a recognized objective of current public policy to encourage as many students as possible to secure some kind of higher education, there are indications that the administration and the provision of financial aid will continue to be an important objective and function of student personnel services in the years ahead.

6. *To help each student develop a sense of individual responsibility and self-discipline.* Symptoms of higher education's failure to develop self-discipline appear vividly to the dean, who has to deal with panty raids, cheating, and sexual misconduct, and to the faculty member who is distressed with the way students choose easy courses and do just enough to get by. Sound personnel practice is based upon the principle that every contact with a student should give that student increased independence and ability to handle future problems on his own. Yet many colleges and universities, in their relations with students, parents, and the public, attempt to assume a degree of responsibility which robs society of an important lesson it must learn if college education is to be truly higher education. That lesson simply is—college students must eventually

grow up, assume certain responsibilities for themselves, and bear the consequences of their behavior. The concept of *in loco parentis* should not lead colleges to assume more authority than the parents themselves would exercise if the students were at home during the comparable four years.

This issue gives rise to the dilemma between the authority exercised by the institution in all its areas and the freedom granted to students. Vice President Haskew of the University of Texas described the situation well when he characterized present practice in higher education as one of:

> . . . such alternation between the practice of authority and the practice of freedom that the student is left with nothing more than rudderless motive power . . . Some schools deal with this issue on the basis of self defense, I fear, championing enough freedom to keep the students reasonably happy and practicing enough authority to keep teachers from resigning. . . .
>
> On three points the protagonists of freedom, the protagonists of authority, and perhaps all the rest of us are agreed. One is that we are not satisfied with the results to date of society's effort to resolve this issue. The second is that the synthesis to be worked out must include elements of both freedom and authority. The third is that a synthesis for schools is integral with a synthesis for the family and for the community.[5]

7. *To interpret university objectives, policies, rules, and administration to students, faculty, alumni, and citizens in general; and to communicate student attitudes, opinions and activities to the faculty and general public.* The activities of colleges and college students are big news. With a larger portion of the college-age population going to college, more and more people have a first-hand interest in what is happening on college campuses. More than ever before, institutions of higher education are obligated to interpret their work and functions to all aspects of society. It is almost a tragedy for higher education that intellectuals as a group have built up a feeling of disdain, if not antagonism, toward the concept of public relations needed in higher education. This disdain has often led to a gulf between students on the one hand and college faculties and administration on the other. Because educators and others fail

---

[5] Laurence D. Haskew, "The Fields Are White Unto Harvest," *Teachers College Record,* LVII, No. 6 (1956), 349.

to inform themselves about student opinions and outlook, a similar gulf has developed between students and the public at large.

The image students have of their institutions and of themselves in general has an important bearing upon their conduct and behavior. In order to make the most of their latent educational potentialities, college students must destroy some misconceptions including: the image held by society that college students are irresponsible youngsters; and the idea that quality education can be attained only in a "selected few" colleges and universities.

A systematic approach to this problem requires the cooperative efforts of all segments of the educational world. Student personnel workers are in a strategic position to advance such a program because they have close relationships with students, parents, high school personnel, and alumni. A superficial image-building campaign will not achieve the desired results. It is important that all persons interested in the higher educational process make the attempt to understand the intricate problems faced by higher education as it serves more people than ever before in the history of the world.

8. *To help create an atmosphere of high morale and loyalty towards the institution.* Much of the disorder and unrest which has been reported on many college campuses arises from the lack of identification of the individual student with his college. Thus a feeling of identification with his own college or university should be provided in order to integrate students and their cultures into the efforts of the total institution. It does not preclude strong criticism of certain phases of the college, nor should it, but it does furnish a positive basis for evaluating differences among and between student groups, for eliminating misunderstandings, and for coordinating efforts toward common objectives.

Size and complexity are not, in themselves, the controlling factors in the students' lack of identification. Rather, the general orientation of the total campus community influences his outlook. The student personnel program plays a unique and important part in determining the prevailing attitude the individual student develops toward his college. Hopefully such attitudes developed will be positive ones.

Basic Principles and Concepts Underlying Student Personnel Work

1. The concept of individuality embraces the fact that students differ from each other in capacities, abilities, interests, aspirations, rate of maturation, and in almost every other conceivable trait. To treat them as if all were identical in their development is to act in ignorance of facts known about human development.

2. A person becomes a free and effective citizen by exercising self-direction and self-restraint rather than by being directed and restrained by some external authority. Responsibility, which necessarily accompanies freedom in a democracy, is most effectively nurtured by encouraging the individual to share in decisions affecting him. That is why student personnel work is not prescriptive in telling students what to do or how to act; but rather it aims to provide guidelines and encouragement for self-direction and allows for voluntary exercise of self-restraint in all individuals.

3. Student personnel services are essentially preventive and positive rather than remedial. They attempt to encourage and assist students to make satisfactory adjustments to their educational objectives, rather than providing therapeutic services *after* maladjustments and crippling problems are revealed. Many factors other than intelligence and prior academic preparation are involved in a student's success in college. Factors preventing a student from reaching his maximum level of ability include emotional difficulties, contradictory demands upon his time and energy, competing values, fears of academic inadequacy, or confusion regarding personal and educational goals.

4. The modern world has become so complex that college students are often required to make choices for which they have had inadequate preparation, experience, or information. The typical method of college instruction, which divides the world of knowledge into artificially created segments, often fails to provide the student with an understanding about the world into which he has to fit or with information necessary to meaningfully relate the various segments of knowledge. The rapidly changing pace of modern society, with its technological developments, social and physical mobility, and disruption of normal relationships, frequently forces individuals into situations in which they need assistance in order to work efficiently.

5. Student personnel workers realize that the individual is affected by a complexity of forces. The students' behavior in its broadest sense is determined by more than just one aspect of the college community. Student personnel workers must establish effective working relationships with faculty members, alumni, parents, news media, and many other sources that make demands upon the individual student. The student personnel worker must assist the individual in recognizing those demands upon him which are legitimate.

6. Effective student personnel service recognizes the role emotions play in human behavior. Some choices are relatively easy to make and cause minimal emotional tension; but difficult or particularly significant choices can create an emotional tension that may affect the individual's ability to make the choice. Increasingly, the college-age group is becoming the focal point for emotional demands resulting from competing ideologies, political views, and value systems. Interacting emotions, often pressured by parental and financial problems, can severely complicate a student's choice of behavior in a particular situation.

7. Since student personnel service believes that the proper social aim is to strive for maximum individual development, the educational institution which accepts a student is professionally obligated to help him become the best student, the best "person," the most effective citizen, and the most productive worker possible, whether he be a genius or "just average." For over one hundred years, American higher education has rejected the idea of serving only a specially selected elite. This policy of providing higher education for the masses has necessitated services and concerns which might not be required in a system catering only to the elite. But even in those institutions serving a very selective student group, personnel services have proven their value because they have assisted individuals in utilizing their abilities and have helped them develop their capabilities to the maximum.

8. Student personnel service is not a discipline in itself, but it synthesizes the findings and procedures from all fields concerned with human behavior. Any attempt to base student personnel service upon *one* discipline excludes valuable insights and information necessary in a broadly effective program. Failure to utilize the rapidly developing field of communication theory on some campuses, for example, has caused striking and abrupt breakdowns in student relations.

Summary

The field of student personnel services in higher education has developed in response to needs and forces arising from changing patterns in American colleges and universities. The services attempt to place the student at the center of his education by emphasizing the unity of the educational process. Its techniques and methods have been developed in order to assist the total institution in its work and to maintain the coherence and integrity of the college environment.

CHAPTER II

Recruitment and Orientation

The sequence of events leading to college enrollment begins with the prospective college student in the ninth grade, or perhaps much earlier for some individuals, and becomes a continuous activity through the total program of higher education. The students' ultimate decision to enroll in a particular program within a specific university or college comes about after he is barraged with pre-college materials, high school visitations, college days, career conferences, college student contacts, testing programs, and college admission procedures. While each of these activities may be very important, college administrators, particularly personnel deans, should be alert to the influence of these pressures, and should recognize the need for an organized approach.

Interpreting Higher Education

Any program which interprets higher education to the public and provides orientation for new students must be based on the understanding that higher education connotes a variety of things to different people. The motivations, aspirations, and expectations of the people interested in higher education help shape their perceptions of college education.

Despite the desires of those engaged in higher education, most college students and the American public see college education in economic terms. To them college means a better paying job, usually a professional job. Stories frequently appear in the popular press and magazines pointing out that every year of education adds dollars to a person's total earnings during his occupational career. It is made clear that college graduates have an advantage over non-college graduates when it comes to entering and progressing in certain professions.

A second major reason students want to go to college falls in the social category—people. Parents and young adults alike see college as an opportunity to meet the right people, and to learn valuable skills in human relations. College provides an opportunity to participate in activities which help an individual develop as a gregarious creature, and help him also gain status in progressing to a higher station in life.

The third reason for going to college is one that educators would prefer to find dominant among students, but, instead, find it is only the minority of students who enter college to fulfill the intellectual and academic aspirations classified as learning. Only the few seek to gain a better understanding of the world, absorb the heritage of knowledge, become discerning in appreciation of art, music, literature, and other cultural aspects of life. Too few students are interested in developing skills and abilities for creative and individual thought.

Therefore a challenge the student personnel service has is to interpret the nature of the *intellectual* gains of higher education when presenting pre-college material to prospective college students and again when indoctrinating students during the college orientation program. The interpretation must be presented in a meaningful manner that can be understood by the students, their parents, and society at large.

There is no question but that society feels a college education is a good and a desirable thing, even if only a short period can be completed.

Fred Hechinger, education editor of *The New York Times,* described the concern of the father of a senior at a boys' preparatory school in Connecticut. The father was determined his son should go to Yale. The college counselor at the prep school pointed out that the boy's scholastic record was not good enough to gain him admittance to Yale and even if he did get in, he would not last six months. "That's all right," said the father, "even if he lasts only six months, he will at least be eligible for membership in the Yale Club."[1]

Particularly conspicuous has been the failure of higher education to interpret effectively to the public at large its role in terms of the increasing *public* benefits derived from a highly educated population. Relatively few people see higher education as a force helping

---

[1] *The New York Times,* July 1, 1962, Sec. 4, p. 7.

a democratic country face the complex problems of a rapidly shrinking world. All too often society discusses admission to college and financial aid to students from the "entrepreneur" point of view, such as investing time and money "now" in order to gain an investment return "later." A better social policy for the country might be that, whether or not an individual wanted to invest and gain a return on his investment, his educational aim should be to seek that kind of education which will develop his potentialities to the greatest degree in order that he become an informed citizen, a leader in society, and a competent voter.

A basic concern of the student personnel worker with regard to pre-college counseling is the quality of information provided prospective students, parents and high school counselors. Courses offered, the mechanics for making application, financial aid programs, requirements for admission, various admission plans, advanced placement opportunities, deadlines for application and other specific, helpful information must be accurately presented and then properly interpreted.

High School Relationships

Colleges and universities need a positive, helpful relationship with high school principals and student counselors, to assist not only in interpreting college to young students, but also in supplying the institution with information about their students.

High school staff members are flooded with various reference forms and application blanks, requiring many different kinds of answers about and diverse evaluations of individual students in both objective and subjective terms. Principals and counselors must cope with national pre-college and college testing programs, many of which are taken early in high school. They must contend with aggressive representatives from colleges and universities, who pursue high quality students with the avidness of an athletic coach seeking a high school All-American for the collegiate team.

Professionally, the college administrator must assume a responsibility assisting in the removal of the mystery and vagueness of recruiting, and in reducing the waste and inefficiency of procedures for entering higher education. A cooperative relationship with high school principals and counselors is, therefore, essential to a successful pre-college interpretation and admissions program.

Of great concern to the student personnel worker is the fact that even though parents of young children want and expect their children to go to college, very few are making adequate provision for the cost of such an experience.

Somehow or other, they feel that enrollment opportunities and financial assistance will always be available. However, based on enrollment projections, there probably will not be sufficient physical capacity in colleges and universities to meet even the minimum needs of the current high school population. Costs will quite probably increase, and parents who see future educational costs in present day terms, and are not preparing for the future, face a rude awakening. The situation poses a great challenge to those charged with the responsibility of interpreting higher education and providing ways and means of participation for the greatest possible number of qualified students.

There is, then, a definite need for some professional and mechanical means whereby colleges can cooperate with high schools in explaining the nature and cost of higher education to parents and students early in high school or even in junior high. Colleges must be alert in interpreting democratic aims to all members of that society wherein they will function—whether or not they anticipate receiving students from any particular group. Students will increasingly come from families which probably have not had any previous college experience; for this reason, the institution of higher education will have to interpret college standards, the role of students, and the role of higher education. The nature of the highly verbal collegiate intellectual process, and the necessity for objective critical thinking regarding higher education, must be understood by all concerned.

Recruitment

Recruitment is a legitimate activity on the part of all institutions of higher education, and a significant aspect of the total process for entry into higher education. Recruitment activities range from the obvious procedures of the admission officers—literature, films, formal speeches, and personal interviews—to the more subtle activities of nearly all members of the college staff, whether it be the president speaking to a service club or a professor judging a high school science fair. Another means of recruitment comes from the students themselves, through a quiet talk with a friend back home or through a campus event to which hundreds of high school seniors have been invited. What is done and said by this wide range of individuals has a major relationship to the recruitment of the right students by the college.

In administering student personnel services the concern should be to assist all parties in the recruitment process and to coordinate all activities in such a way that what is said or written rings with authenticity. Oftentimes the recruiting program puts emphasis upon social activities, athletics, vocational orientation, and the like, thereby downgrading the prevailing intellectuality of the student body.

College entrance has become a standard part of American life. One has only to look through current magazines and newspapers, talk with young people in any setting, or eavesdrop on talk at the bridge table to realize that the general public is greatly concerned with gaining admittance to college and earning a degree. Yet it cannot be accepted as fact that parents and prospective students know what college is all about. Some feel that their only concern is to choose a college and the applicant will be accepted. But gaining entrance to college and earning a degree has become such a complex process and has created such diverse problems that accurate information must be disseminated to both parents and students to properly inform them of the requirements.

Determining Admission Policy and Procedures

As in so many other student personnel services, there is no single best method for organizing the institutional resources for successful admission practice. All segments of the academic community have a legitimate interest in admissions policy procedures. In addition, parents, alumni, high school officials, and the public at large feel quite properly that they should have a voice in determining who should go to college.

In general, the typical college has an admissions committee chaired by the director of admissions and composed of representatives of various administrative offices, student services, and faculty members. Its function is not to determine specific cases of admission, but rather to determine broad admissions policy, based upon the dominant institutional characteristics. Much misunderstanding stems from vague admissions policies and an inadequate statement of the educational goals of the institution. More than that, the admissions committee must take a hard look at the continual pressure on an institution presenting itself as being something other than what it is. From an educational point of view, admissions policy should not necessarily change just because there are more applicants one year than the next. To meet the demand for a minimum number of students, the criteria for selection are inevitably, and perhaps unfortunately, related to the volume of applications for admission at any given date.

Representation on the admissions committee should reflect an over-all institutional unity of faculty-student-administrative relationships. The level and quality of classroom teaching are at stake in the admissions process. Furthermore, the tone of the college community is reflected by the degree to which the faculty member is student-oriented, and feels himself to be a part of the student selection procedure. The presence of students on the admissions committee is not a common practice in higher education. However, advocates of participation in this committee by all aspects of the college community propose that student representatives could play a significant role in the determination and implementation of admissions procedures. The responsibility of the admissions committee includes the soliciting and the coordinating of the efforts and contributions of all persons concerned with the admissions and recruitment process.

Selection of Applicants

In recent years popular literature has been replete with exaggerated stories of closed college doors. The number of qualified applicants is so great that it is important to remove misconceptions and to eliminate mystery and suspicion regarding the admissions process.

It is a fact that the degree of ambiguity in its requirements is indicative of a college's selectivity.[2] The less selective an institution

---

[2] Henry S. Dyer, "Ambiguity in Selective Admissions," *The Journal of the Association of College Admissions Counselors,* IX, No. 2 (1963), 15.

is the more specific it can be in its admission policy. A high school student, by checking his state university's college catalog, should generally be able to determine his eligibility and thus estimate his chances for admission. In contrast, it is much more difficult for even an outstanding high school student to know whether or not he will gain admittance to a typically selective liberal arts college under private control, even though he may have what appears to be the exact record which the college recommends for applying students.

From the personnel point of view, it is important that counselors at all levels of education work with students and parents in interpreting the admissions process. This is an essential part of the pre-college counseling done by college representatives and the high school.

Currently, most institutions use three sources of information in selecting students: (1) the scholastic record from high school including rank in class and courses taken, (2) the results of one or more tests taken upon direction of the college or taken voluntarily to strengthen the application, and (3) personal data gathered from an extensive application blank, from references by high school principals, or from an interview with an admissions counselor.

From a procedural point of view, most institutions place major weight on the scholastic rank in high school. While the testing programs are becoming increasingly popular and widespread, they still are generally of secondary significance to the field of higher education. Many specific institutions, however, place great weight upon the results of tests. The tests range from a specified national program, such as those of the College Entrance Examination Board or of the American College Testing Program, to specific diagnostic or achievement tests. Most of the information requested is used to help the credentials analyst determine whether the high school achievement record is a valid indicator of the student's potential to do satisfactory work at the college level.

A significant development in higher education has been the use of various types of achievement tests to give students advanced standing in college, with or without credit. For example, a high school student who has done particularly well in a language and has, perhaps, had study abroad may take a language achievement test and be placed in a junior level course in college. He may receive as many as six or eight hours of actual college credit prior to entrance to college.

Personal data from interviews are used primarily to complement information from the application blank or from the scholastic records and test results.

The actual selection of applicants is an individual institutional concern. Liberal arts colleges, technical institutes, and specialized schools may vary considerably in their entrance requirements. The college administrator must convey to the student an understanding of the selection procedures and the admission requirements of his particular institution.

Admission Process and Procedures

The current situation of expanding enrollments and the involvement of many agencies in working with youth have fortunately brought about a re-examination of the entire process by which students gain admission to institutions of higher learning. The educational buyers' market allows some institutions an opportunity to align admission objectives and procedures with sound educational philosophy, policy, and practice. When the very survival of the institution depends upon "recruiting" a sufficient number of students to meet the budget, it is difficult indeed for the educational point of view to prevail.

The actual admission processes in colleges and universities range from complicated, time-consuming procedures to simply "signing on the dotted line." Some select colleges require prospective students to be interviewed by alumni. Parents are interviewed by admissions counselors in the home, and one or more campus visitations by the applicant are required. At the other extreme, some institutions permit "walk-ins," in which a student, who first appears on the day of registration, is given conditional admission pending the submission of a high school transcript attesting to the accuracy of his statements. From the student personnel point of view, the admission process is basically important to subsequent success in college. The admission of students to college or university education should be based on the belief that the educational experience will benefit the individual. Careful consideration should be given to the prospective students' past performance, his objectives, and to the purposes of the institution. There should be reasonable expectation that the student has the ability necessary to succeed. Since it is student personnel that is concerned with the welfare of the student, close liaison must be maintained with all correlated personnel offices, both in high school and college. Student inadequacies as well as strengths should be made known to the campus agencies if they are to assist the student in reaching maximum growth.

All these concerns must be related to the individual student: his goals, motivations, potentialities, level of achievement, and all traits which make up his total personality.

The Orientation Process

The major purpose of orientation to higher education is to communicate to the new student that college is a self-directed, intellectually oriented experience. Purposes next in importance include informing the student and his parents about the college, counseling them, completing various mechanical processes needed to enroll the student in his classes, and, in general, getting the new student off to the best possible start in his new career.

Effective orientation is more important currently than at any time in the history of higher education because of the increasing heterogeneity of student bodies, complicated educational programs requiring a greater variety of choices, and greater confusion in the minds of the general public regarding higher education. Greater depth in academic preparation and wider socio-economic backgrounds, facilitating travel and familiarity with college organizations, are reasons for this increased heterogeneity. Nevertheless, it must be remembered that while some students will know a great deal about college and its life, others will be completely mystified by its terminology and differences.

The more competent a student body, the more important an effective orientation. This anomaly rises from the fact that competent students often have wide ranges of interests and can succeed in a wide variety of programs—increased honors programs, advanced placement, freshman seminars, special sections, and extra credit arrangements. The choices these students are required to make are as burdensome to them as choices are to less qualified students. Furthermore, competent students need particularly to be channelled in the direction of establishing high academic and intellectual standards for themselves. They need to have emphasized for them the degree of self-discipline and self-direction true scholarship requires.

In all too many institutions the orientation program has been considered "new student week." Unfortunately, they have often been "dis-orientation" weeks instead of orientation weeks. The new freshman is given tests, told about the health service, escorted through the library, and addressed by various academic officials. He is introduced to extra-curricular activities, taught the school song and yells, inducted into groups for special messages from student leaders, and, in some colleges, run through fraternity or sorority rush. A short time later, he is counseled by faculty advisers, and then enlisted into hundreds of different classes by a process called registration and enrollment. Frequently this is a traumatic experience in itself. None of the activities or programs listed above is, in itself, bad; together, however, they often have given the student a biased, chaotic, and distorted perception of higher education.

The importance of orientation demands a critical re-evaluation by student personnel workers of their orientation programs in the light of changing institutional and student needs. Moreover, the entire institution should be utilized to show that, in addition to the procedural and socially pleasant experiences of college life, there will be academic demands upon the student—there will be high scholastic achievement standards to meet, greater personal qualities to develop, high moral values as well as ethical standards to attain from a full college experience.

Since orientation is a process of communication, a number of significant lessons from communication research should be applied when developing, conducting, and evaluating a particular program. Some of these are:

1. Meaning is conveyed in a number of ways, not just through what is said. Thus, its methods and procedures will communicate as much about a college as what is verbalized.

2. The orientation process begins with the first pre-college contact and continues thereafter. It includes what is written in news stories, catalogues, brochures, and letters, as well as what is included in formal orientation material.

3. Fellow students and friends are more influential in communication about the college than are written statements of faculty

and administrative representatives. Nevertheless, the appeal of the intellectual and academic life *must* overcome conflicting or contradictory appeals from the many student sub-cultures in the campus community.

4. What is to be communicated by any single program or procedure must be as clear, precise, and specific as possible. It is difficult to make an academic appeal at a pep session or social mixer.

5. The essential meaning of orientation must be presented in so outstanding a manner that it will immediately stand out from the many messages with which the new student is deluged. The wonders of the college world speak with many voices and with a wide variety of appeals. To be successful, the appeal of the dean for academic purpose must compete (by using proper status appeals, timing, language, and sheer force) with the allure of the beauty queen or the prestige of the "Big Man on Campus."

6. Individuals respond to new experiences in terms of prior experience and in relation to their needs and interests. A message, therefore, must be in approximately the same language as that used by its intended recipients. Further, it must not conflict too much with the individual's previous experience. A student who has always "gotten by" with minimum effort in high school will not be particularly receptive to warnings that he will have to work hard in college; he has heard the same message before and his experience robs it of significance. The application of this principle means that students will study harder when they are required to do so by class assignments, and not as a result of efforts to keep them from indulging in frivolous activity.

7. The appeal for maximum achievement is most effective when it arouses personality needs in the student and suggests ways to meet those needs. All individuals have basic needs such as that for security, status, freedom from constraint, understanding, and love. The most effective appeal will be the one which motivates and suggests methods to meet such needs. Fear of failure is one of the strongest appeals currently used. Research and experience, however, have demonstrated the greater strength of appeals to status, self-fulfillment, and personal worth.

8. The responses to stimuli of most individuals are made in a group context. Group approval, therefore, is significant in determining an individual's response to any particular appeal. For ex-

ample, exhortation to enroll in superior student or honors sections of particular courses may go unheeded if the prevailing feeling is negative. For this and other reasons the practice of dividing new students into groups, with students as group leaders, is sound. These groups, however, as well as the more permanent and persuasive groups on the campus, must be carefully analyzed and consciously considered in designing the orientation program. Failure to consider them may result in a weakened if not actually undermined positive emphasis.

9. The follow-up to the formal orientation program is vitally important if the students are to receive any lasting value from it. The most effective follow-up consists of a conscious effort on the part of the professors to relate in their opening classes the sum and substance of the orientation messages. Professors can aid their students by reviewing study methods, by emphasizing expectancies of the college, and by relating their specific course to the general body of knowledge it represents. In many colleges the opening day of class is lost time if all that the professor does is name a textbook and make a routine assignment.

Summary

The specific content and activities of an orientation program are not as important as the degree to which the resources of the total institution are mobilized to effectively communicate the essential nature and demands of the college. Communication about the nature of college must begin early in a student's educational life and must continue through his college days. Recruitment, admission, and orientation must be a coordinated process which emphasizes to the new student that his college career will be a highly demanding one, requiring active self-direction not merely passive cooperation. Such clarification of underlying principles should help eliminate many of the student problems currently encountered on campuses.

CHAPTER III

Financial Aid

Financial aid usually consists of scholarships, loans, grants, and jobs. Despite variations in definition and methods, all kinds of monetary assistance provided to college students are classified as financial aid, and consequently are of concern to student personnel administrators. College-administered financial aid is on the rise, but students, parents, colleges, and society at large use a wide variety of methods to meet the all too familiar gap between available financial resources and the cost of securing a college education.

Student financial assistance began, as did many other aspects of American higher education, with the founding of Harvard College, where the first bell ringer was a student who received a portion of his expenses. From this modest origin, financial aid has grown to an estimated $447,000,000 in 1960 and an astonishing $1,903,560,000 has been predicted by 1970. When one considers the multiple details of policy formulation, application processing, inquiries, scores of calculations, award procedures, collection schedules, repayment records, and follow-up practices, it is easy to understand why the administration of financial aid has grown in importance from being merely an added duty to being a major responsibility for student personnel officers.

The fact that only in recent years has the administration of financial aid been delegated to specialized personnel reflects the chaotic and tardy state of the nation's aid efforts. No comprehensive purpose or philosophy guided aid efforts until well after World War II and the G.I. Bill. Even today financial aid is used for a wide variety of purposes ranging from government support for educational institutions to public relations and recruiting.

Financial aid has made a positive transition from a highly inconsistent, personalized process into a business-like operation serving and satisfying the student, the institution and the public. Numerous factors have forced educational administrators, businessmen, and government officials to formulate a philosophy assuring equitable treatment of individuals in addition to deriving the greatest social good from the vast sums involved. Among these factors are the increased importance of financial aid as a significant aspect of higher educational policy; its complex nature results from broad objectives, lengthening repayment periods, and its sheer growth in dollar volume.

Society's goals of equality and opportunity, efficient productivity, and democratic education have forced this careful attention. The student personnel administrator holds the responsibility of leading his institution into the era of sound practice.

The recent increases in external sources of financial aid have not reduced the college's involvement in its administration. Its role has changed, however, because it is now frequently handling money which is not its own and, consequently, bears a greater responsibility than ever before for efficient, equitable administration. Increasing amounts from state and federal sources, non-profit loan funds, business foundations, and private sources require new ideas as well as ingenious and intelligent responses to the many new problems and philosophical issues. To answer the need, there is more definite agreement on principles for administration of financial aid, a growing number of professional specialists who recognize the importance and problems of the field, and an increasing number of techniques for gathering and interpreting information essential to a sound program.

A Centralized Function

Regardless of the size of the institution, student aid should be a centralized function. Experience has clearly demonstrated that institutional responsibilities and the needs of the individual cannot be met when a variety of personnel and other offices act independently of each other under inconsistent and contradictory policies. There is a need for total institutional involvement in all financial aid policies. Otherwise, fragmented administration of aid is only wasteful and self-defeating.

A central office or agency can best achieve the broad objectives of student aid when it administers and coordinates all student services and financial resources provided by the institution. These services include jobs, loans, special housing placement, fee remissions, discounts, and grants. This office should also serve as a clearing house providing information about student needs to groups and individuals outside the college who desire to make awards to students—churches, clubs, business organizations, charitable foundations, wealthy individuals, and dedicated alumni. Such a centralized agency would be of great administrative assistance, as well, since it would eliminate delays and assure fair treatment of the student in the light of his needs and the resources of the institution.

Approximately 500 colleges participating in the College Scholarship Service have developed the following guiding principles as the basis for their individual policies and procedures:

1. The primary purpose of a college's financial aid program should be to provide financial assistance to students who, without such aid, would be unable to attend the college.
2. Financial assistance consists of scholarships, loans, and employment, which may be offered to students singly or in various combinations.
3. The family of a student is to make a maximum effort to assist the student with college expenses. Financial assistance from colleges and other sources should be viewed only as supplementary to the efforts of the family.
4. In selecting students with need to receive financial assistance, the college should place primary emphasis upon their academic achievement, character, and future promise.
5. The total amount of financial assistance offered a student by a college and by other sources should not exceed the amount he needs.
6. In determining the extent of a student's financial need, the college should take into account the financial support which may be expected from the income, assets, and other resources of the parents and the student.
7. In estimating the amount that a student's family can provide for college expenses, the college should consider the factors that affect a family's financial strength: current income, assets, number of dependents, other educational expenses, debts, retirement needs. In addition, it should consider such special problems as those confronting widows and families in which both parents work.
8. A student who needs financial aid should provide a reasonable part of the total amount required to meet college costs by accepting employment, or a loan, or both. Acceptance of a loan, however, should not be considered by the college as a pre-requisite to the award of a scholarship or job.
9. Because the amount of financial assistance awarded usually reflects the financial situation of the student's family, a public announcement of the amount by the college is undesirable.

10. Consultation between colleges on the kind and amount of financial assistance to be offered a mutual candidate should be encouraged, since this assures relatively equal aid offers to the student, making it possible for him to choose a college on educational rather than financial grounds. This benefits both the student and the college.

11. The college should clearly state the total yearly cost of attendance and should outline for each student seeking assistance an estimate of his financial need.

12. The college should review its financial assistance awards annually and adjust them if necessary in type and amount to reflect changes in the financial needs of students and the cost of attending the institution, as well as to carry out the college's clearly stated policies on upper-class renewals.

13. The college itself should make every effort, and should cooperate with schools and other colleges, to encourage college attendance by all able students.

14. The college should strive, through its publications and other communications, to provide schools, parents and students with factual information about its aid opportunities, programs, and practices.[1]

Despite the program which has been made recently in integrating all aspects of financial aid into a manageable whole, many policies and procedures remain which need intensive and critical examination by student personnel administrators.

The Financial Aid Package

A new concept, growing in acceptance, is that of the "aid package" which combines a scholarship, a loan, and a job in order to meet the student's financial requirements as well as to extend institutional resources as far as possible. For example, an institution, having determined that a student needs $1200, might offer him a $400 scholarship, a $300 loan, and part-time employment for which he would earn $500 during the school year. The rationale of this concept is to meet the student's need through a variety of resources, thus lessening the burden on any one resource. In addition, this plan increases the student's participation in meeting his need.

Most individuals prefer a scholarship to a loan; it is not unreasonable, however, to expect needy students and their families to borrow to some extent in order to help finance an education. In

[1] Reprinted with permission from *College Financial Aid Principles,* published in 1962 by the College Entrance Examination Board, New York.

fact, it has been estimated that in the future, borrowing, whether by student or parents, may well be the major source of funds for advanced schooling.[2] Although it is true that too much work interferes with a student's academic activity, employment when properly balanced, as in the aid package, complements and extends other resources without interfering in the objectives of the student or the institution.

Moon has suggested[3] that students who need $450 or less be offered a low interest loan. Those who require $500 to $900 would be offered a loan of $500 and a job paying the rest, while those needing more than $900 would receive a scholarship or grant for the remainder of the amount. These figures are merely suggestive but illustrate use of multiple sources for the achievement of assistance to a maximum number of students from the resources available. The proportion within a package of each resource may vary to be compatible with the student's situation. An upper classman, because he has demonstrated an ability to survive college competition and has adjusted to college demands, could be expected to borrow and work more than a freshman. Students should not be forced to accept one part of the package in order to receive the others, but the other amounts should not be increased if a student declines one or more of its components.

Honor and Recognition

A troublesome problem facing policy makers of student aid programs is the awarding of scholarships to honor academic achievement, rather than to fulfill the primary objective of financial assistance. The current trend emphasizes the need factor, with a requirement of academic proficiency. There has not, however, been wide acceptance of this view by either the academic community or by society at large. The practice of awarding even small stipends with

---

[2] Dexter M. Keezer, ed., *Financing Higher Education 1960–70* (New York: McGraw-Hill Book Company, Inc., 1959), p. 8.

[3] Rexford G. Moon, Jr., "Some Suggestions Concerning Aid Activities Colleges and Universities," paper given at a Workshop on Financial Aid, sponsored by the American College Personnel Association, Western Interstate Commission for Higher Education and the College Scholarship Service, University of Colorado, Boulder, Colorado, 1964.

honorary scholarships to recognize scholastic proficiency is being questioned because the sum total of even small stipends might enable one or more needy students to secure a college education. The student personnel administrator has the task, therefore, of devising other kinds of honorary recognition, such as bestowing titles —"university fellow," "presidential scholar"; or giving special privileges—access to honors library room, stack privileges in library; or providing special academic recognition—honors courses, special seminars.

Ethics in Financial Aid

In the concepts and principles of the foregoing discussion it is assumed that the student and his parents have honestly reported their ability, or lack of it, to finance a college education. Credit checks and references have been used to approach the problem of those who falsify or honestly underestimate their economic status. Some institutions which use parents' confidential financial statements request copies of recent federal tax forms. The university attempts to gain a reasonable estimate of the educational cost contribution potential of the student and his family. On the other hand, the student has the right to expect complete honesty from the college regarding the terms and conditions of its offer, repayment provisions if the student withdraws from school, etc.

Another area of strain in ethical relations is that of inter-institutional interests. Attempts to outbid for special students, awarding of undercover aid, special payments to athletes, exploitation of gifted or talented students, and irregularities in graduate student stipends, all raise ethical questions which presumably should not need review in the ideal community of scholars.

A third problem relates to increasing services as provided by recent federal legislation and fulfilling society's expectations of higher education. Ethical questions in this area might well be raised concerning the best use of government funds, expenditures for athletes and entertainers, variety of costs for certain students, and the recruiting of the student who has assurances of financial aid.

Administration of State and Federal Programs

Many educational administrators feel that the individual colleges and universities are best qualified to administer state or federal student aid programs. They advocate grants to the institution which would then process applications and distribute funds in the same manner as they would their institutional monies. Others feel, however, that a state commission representing all institutions and all geographic areas is best qualified to do this. Certainly, institutional or regional self-interest should not be a dominant factor in any program. First-hand knowledge of the needs of both student and institution and actual relationship with the student community strongly favor institutional administration under the broad policies established by governing legislation. The student personnel administrator must be knowledgeable about the various financial aid practices in order to contribute to the formulation of an institutional position which meets the objectives of any aid program.

Counseling in Financial Aid

In addition to helping the student and his parents understand the kinds of resources available and providing the necessary information, the financial aid officer should offer empathetic understanding about the high cost of education. The student and his parents should be assisted in understanding the concept of financial need and the selection of methods best adapted to their own earnings and assets.

Another aspect of financial aid counseling is helping the student develop a sense of responsibility to the source of aid. This would be more important with long term loans, but in any case, it would require the student's understanding of the terms of the aid: loan, work, or scholarship.

In counseling about financial problems, the student personnel administrator has the unique ability to alleviate the problem of the student. This, however, is not justification for the forcing or eliminating of certain forms of aid. It merely emphasizes the importance of helping clients decide what will best alleviate the financial burden of higher education.

Sources of Information for Student Borrowers

Perhaps the largest source of student loans (1565 participating institutions) is the National Defense Student Loan Program, Title II. It provides funds to an institution, which, in turn, acts as agent in distribution and collection. The low interest, extended repayment loan program has been expanded by recent changes in legislation. There is now provision for a special Health Professions Student Loan Program encompassing medicine, dentistry, optometry, and nursing. Information can be obtained from the United States Office of Education, Washington, 25, D.C.

The United Student Aid Funds, Inc., is a non-profit corporation organized to provide resources for higher education through school and bank cooperation. Loans are obtained through "hometown" banks with the approval of the college and the corporation, and are repaid to the bank on an extended basis. The Executive Office is located at 845 Third Avenue, New York, New York 10022.

Guaranty programs, similar in operation to the United Student Aid Funds, Inc., may be found in Louisiana, Maryland, Massachusetts, Maine, Michigan, New Hampshire, New Jersey, New York, North Carolina, Ohio, Pennsylvania, Rhode Island, Tennessee, Vermont, and Virginia.

The American Medical Association has a loan program for medical students with all funds originating in one bank. Guaranty is provided by the AMA.

North Dakota has a bank loan program for its students and Wisconsin students may borrow from the State Welfare Department. Several colleges and universities participate in the Henry Strong Eductaional Loan Foundation, the Pickett and Hatcher Educational Fund, Columbus, Georgia, and numerous other private plans. The Methodist Church and many other church denominations as well as public and private sources have student loan programs designed to reduce the financial burden of higher education.

Summary

Financial aid has grown from its historical position as a modest facet of institutional policy to an instrument of national and social importance. This development is the result of a positive effort to remove economic barriers to higher education; much, however, remains to be done. A major challenge facing educational administrators—specifically student personnel administrators—is to lead and stimulate the discussion of philosophical issues, to develop and cultivate resources, and to refine of procedures in order to increase the worth and effectiveness of financial aid as a part of the total educational program.

CHAPTER IV

Counseling Services

Counseling in institutions of higher education in the United States is a general service provided by the total faculty, as well as a specialized function of student personnel. By no means can counseling services be considered tangential to the educative activity of the academic departments; rather they must be thought of as an integral part of a student's total education. A philosophy commonly termed "the student personnel point of view" emphasizes the development of optimal educational experiences for the student through awareness of individual differences, encouragement of self-understanding, and application of appropriate problem-solving techniques. While all faculty members must aid students in the use of their talents and the resources of the institution, the major responsibility for coordinating, initiating, and maintaining counseling services rests with a specialized core of counselors within the student personnel division.

The term "counseling" has been used to describe a wide range of interpersonal relationships on the college campus, and considerable confusion has resulted for students seeking assistance. Although some misunderstanding still exists within the student personnel service, counseling is understood basically to include services performed by professionally trained individuals in assisting students, or others, with decision-making processes. Wrenn points out the difference between the term "counseling" as a specific individualized experience and the broader aspects of student personnel service or guidance, by offering the following definition:

> Counseling is a dynamic and purposeful relationship between two people in which procedures vary with the nature of the student's needs but in which there is always mutual participation by counselor and student with the focus upon self-clarification and self-determination by the student. Within this definition, counseling can be observed in a wide variety of campus situations and must

be understood as existing in both formal and informal services at different levels of specialization.[1]

The services subsumed under the general label of counseling are diverse. In discussing counseling services within the framework of student personnel work, Williamson pinpoints this problem:

> The techniques of counseling individual students may be observed, in greatly modified form, in the individualized services for such problems as off campus housing; granting loans and scholarships; handling discipline cases; assignment of rooms and selection of roommates in dormitories; advising on student activities and programs; helping students choose vocational objectives; selecting optional courses of study; learning to read at college rate and comprehension. Techniques, function, emphasis, and method are to be found in all types of service which deal with progress toward the goals selected by students, viewed as unique individuals.[2]

Counseling, then, is given in various forms and involves a wide range of skills and specialization. The numerous student personnel agencies utilizing counseling techniques are discussed in subsequent chapters; therefore, the counseling services to be considered in the remainder of this chapter are those provided by professional counselors within the confines of the college counseling center and those performed by non-student personnel staff members or agencies.

Counseling–A Frame of Reference

Until very recently, counseling services in colleges and universities were relatively unique to institutions in the United States. A growing democratic concern for the individual as a person has played a major part in the development of counseling services in this country. Counseling is based on an appreciation of the rights, dignity, and worth of the individual, and on his right to develop his personal resources to the fullest. Our democratic society recognizes the right of the individual to accept or reject aid in his decision-making; therefore, counseling is a voluntary process which lends assistance to those making personal adjustments and seeking better self-understanding and self-direction.

---

[1] C. Gilbert Wrenn, *Student Personnel Work in College* (New York: Ronald Press, 1951), p. 60.

[2] E. G. Williamson, *Student Personnel Services in Colleges and Universities* (New York: McGraw-Hill Book Company, 1961), p. 180.

In providing individualized services for students, counselors must be especially understanding of the dynamics of human behavior and must be skilled in communicating with students. While various schools or theories of counseling exist and present interesting and thought-provoking positions for the would-be counselor, there are certain commonalities which will help in gaining a better understanding of the counseling process.

Cottle considers five elements as basic or common to counseling. He states that counselors develop a relationship with the student based on mutual trust, confidence, and respect. This relationship requires the acceptance of the student for what he is and a belief in his ultimate ability to resolve his own problem.

A second element is communication, in its broad sense, between the counselor and the client. This implies an awareness of feelings, attitudes, and emotions, and the expression and understanding of these concerns.

Knowledge of human behavior, and understanding form a third common dimension of counseling. This is gained by the counselor's integration of his academic training with his varied experiences.

A fourth common element concerns the change in feelings expressed by the client as he progresses in counseling; his developing insight into the nature of his difficulty and his graduate approach to the solution of his own problems.

The fifth element is structuring in the counseling situation. This is simply a development of "ground rules" and clarifies the process regarding roles and responsibilities.[3]

Although these common elements cannot capture the intricacies of counseling, they do provide a broad framework for understanding the basic procedures involved in the process.

An examination of the commonalities leads to the realization that counseling can exist at many levels and may be practiced by a wide variety of people. Counseling has developed, however, into a specialized field, and is generally thought of as requiring professional training.

---

[3] W. C. Cottle, "Some Common Elements in Counseling," *Personnel and Guidance Journal* (1953), pp. 4–8.

The Development of Specialization

Historically, counseling services grew out of the need for greater specialization than could be effectively offered by other educational specialists. Several factors combined to force such specialization.

The educator of yesterday was a generalist. He knew a great deal about a wide variety of subjects and often taught students individually or in small groups. The development of ideas and the solving of problems could easily be accomplished through personal interchange as the professor was well acquainted with his students. Professional competencies were easily maintained by regularly reading the limited publications or by attending annual professional meetings.

With scientific advances in given fields, however, the body of knowledge in those areas increased to the point where a teacher could no longer remain expert in all fields, and necessarily confined himself to smaller and smaller limits of knowledge. When problems and inquiries arose in other areas, the newly established specialist found it necessary to refer students to the specialists in those areas.

The increase in the size of institutional enrollments also contributed to the establishment of separate counseling services. As teaching loads increased and small classes gave way to mass education, it became practically impossible for teachers to engage students in individual discussions, to develop an understanding of every student, or to devote unlimited time to individual problems. The teacher found it increasingly difficult to know his students and their problems and thus looked for assistance. Counseling of students, based on a foundation of knowledge about individual students and their behavior, grew as a specialty.

The growth of counseling specialization also relates to the complexity of decision-making in modern day living. The educational and vocational structure of fifty years ago was sufficiently simple to permit selection of courses or occupations without much difficulty, and little attention was given to the degree of compatibility between choices and individual characteristics. Changes in plans were not too disruptive because there was a limited number of possible careers, and errors or omissions were easily corrected. The college catalog prescribed the requirements for graduation and the selection of optional courses was extremely limited. Academic advising was relatively routine. Vocational counseling was concerned with the professional areas of medicine, law, or the ministry, or to occupations found within the surrounding community.

Today, however, careful planning and consideration must be given to decision-making in order to avoid costly mistakes. A typical large college or university will offer thousands of courses leading to academic majors in a vast number of different areas. The world of work is composed of some 40,000 occupations, with new specialty fields being added yearly. The complexity of educational and vocational decision-making places tremendous demands upon the present generation which needs counseling assistance.

The large cross-section of the general public, represented in most colleges, reflects the confusion and uncertainty of the general population with regard to their future, their vocational careers, their role as citizens, and their role as individuals in a somewhat chaotic society. It is this uncertain atmosphere that leads to today's college student's needs for counsel.

Testing

Since the beginning of intelligence measurement by Alfred Binet in 1905, testing has grown to the extent that the average college or university student is subjected to many kinds of psychological evaluations during his scholastic career. Essentially, tests are no more than a short sample of human behavior, used to predict future behavior or assess present competence in certain areas. As such, tests play an important role in counseling today. The terms "College Boards," "National Merit," "Strong," "Kuder," or "MMPI" are commonly used in the counseling of normal individuals. The specific use of tests in counseling has been a controversial subject by proponents of the various theories of counseling, but their use is a generally accepted fact. Tests are not toys for the amusement of counselors, but instruments designed to aid in helping clients gain a better understanding of their personal resources.

Used as tools in the assessment of individual capabilities, tests are usually classified within one of four general areas.

1. *The Assessment of Abilities (aptitudes).* The relativity of the strength the individual has in areas of learning ability or skills of a specific nature plays a predominate role in the determination of

potential. Within the collegiate setting, the primary concern is with the student's ability to profit from his educational experience.

Appraisal techniques have been developed which attempt to assess a student's potential learning capacity. Numerous tests of this nature are administered by national testing agencies and the results are sent to various colleges where they are used as one of several criteria for college admission. Other tests, administered on the campus, may be used in individual counseling to aid the student in gaining a better understanding of his ability to compete successfully in various areas of academic pursuit.

Although tests of general learning ability or collegiate aptitude are probably the most widely used, other kinds of measurements have been developed to assess learning potential in various other areas. These range from mechanical and clerical aptitude testing to such specific areas as aptitudes for medical and legal professions. When used by a skilled counselor who understands the limits of tests, such instruments can serve a valuable purpose, but in and of themselves, tests cannot tell the total story of success and failure. Fortunately or unfortunately, factors other than ability are necessary for gaining an understanding of the future adjustment of the typical college student.

2. *The Assessment of Achievement.* Every college or university requires the prospective student to submit a transcript of courses and credits for evaluation before being accepted for enrollment. This document helps determine placement within the various subject areas offered by the institution. Just as individuals vary in their ability to profit from educational experiences, so do educational institutions vary in the nature of their course offerings. In order to determine the level of proficiency of students in specific areas of study, and thus aid in placement of them within the university, many colleges and universities require students to take achievement tests in different subjects. The results of these and other tests can be beneficial in informing the student how his achievement relates to other students with similar experiences.

3. *The Measurement of Interests.* As important in the attainment of educational goals as ability and past achievement are, the importance of the student's interest in pursuing and studying a particular subject or in selecting a specific goal cannot be discounted.

The work of Strong[4] clearly points to the relationship of interest patterns to various kinds of occupations. Research by Berdie[5] indicates considerable differentiation of various patterns of academic concentration and interest profiles. The assessment of these various occupational interests plays an important part, not only in educational and vocational decision-making, but also in determining life goals. Interest inventories, most frequently used in individual counseling, attempt to determine the relative strengths or weaknesses of vocational interests in relation to the assumed characteristics of some hypothetical worker or to the patterns of interests scored by actual workers within given occupations. The results of such inventories often serve to focus attention on areas in which individual students seem to have interests usually associated with specific occupational fields, or at the least, initiate interest in occupational and educational exploration.

4. *The Appraisal of Personality or Adjustment.* Recently, psychologists and counselors have come under attack by those who consider the use of personality assessment techniques an "invasion of privacy." Many counselors, however, believe that an individual exists as a total person, and that if assistance is to be given, it is necessary to develop an understanding of the total person. While speaking of a trend in the vocational guidance movement, which might apply equally well to the total field of counseling, Thompson states that the movement is characterized by increasing recognition of (1) the complexity of factors affecting everyday life decisions and (2) the fact that an individual's vocational goals, and the behaviors leading toward those goals, are an expression of the total person, not merely of a compartmentalized segment of the individual.[6]

At present, personality assessment techniques are used in individual counseling to aid the student in gaining a better understanding of the various feelings, attitudes, and motivations which serve, at least in part, as determiners of his present and future behavior. The assessment of personality is an extremely difficult process,

---

[4] E. K. Strong, Jr., *Vocational Interests 18 Years After College* (Minneapolis: University of Minnesota Press, 1955).

[5] R. F. Berdie, "Aptitude, Achievement, Interest, and Personality Tests: A Longitudinal Comparison," *Journal of Applied Psychology* (1955), pp. 103–114.

[6] Albert S. Thompson, "Personality Dynamics and Vocational Counseling," *Personnel and Guidance Journal,* XXXVIII (1960), pp. 350–357.

shrouded in considerable uncertainty because of the complexity of human behavior. The knowledge gained by personality assessment has little meaning by itself, and must be carefully considered in relation to the information gained through other counseling techniques.

Other testing programs. The counseling center will frequently be called upon to assist with testing activities for other divisions of the university. Tests administered by the center often extend beyond those needed in the counseling of individual students. The counselor's special knowledge of testing makes him a valuable resource to the admission's office, and the center may be involved in administering and interpreting tests to entering students. The scholarship office may seek help in screening scholarship applicants through the use of tests. Various academic departments will depend upon the counseling center to assist in giving placement and advanced standing examinations to their students. Some professors seek consultation in developing tests for their courses, and utilize the test scoring services of the center.

The administration of tests often extends beyond the university. Many counseling centers enter into contractual agreements to do the testing for independent school systems, for private agencies, or for local companies. Such services may include any of the types of testing described above.

Specialized Counseling Services

The role of counseling specialists will vary considerably from institution to institution, but will always be concerned with students who are experiencing difficulties in making adjustments to educational, vocational, or personal-social problems. The dynamic nature of both human behavior and the personal adjustment process makes it difficult to apply any taxonomy to individual counseling problems.

The majority of counselors are well aware of the dangers and limitations inherent in the prevailing methods of classifying problem areas. These broad labels are used only as a means to discuss problems, procedures, and outcomes of counseling. With these limitations of the inter-relatedness of human problems in mind, attention will be directed to these specific classifications of problems as faced by the professional counselor.

Educational counseling. The very nature of the educational enterprise, and the setting for the vast majority of counseling, makes it appropriate that the primary concern of the counselor be centered upon student concerns in the area of education. Although distribution of the work load is dependent upon the nature of record keeping, it appears that problems of an educational nature comprise approximately one third of the counselor's total counseling time. Undoubtedly, the complexity of courses and major subject fields contributes greatly to the decision-making problems of students. Most counselors, however, find that their work involves a more basic problem—that of assisting the student in developing realistic educational plans and in locating the various resources of the college or university that will aid him in attaining his objectives. Admittedly, individuals should go to college because of their intellectual curiosity and their desire for intellectual achievement. The fact is, however, that very few college students today initially come to a college campus for this reason. Most students enter college because of parental expectation, prestige factors, social pressures, or for strict vocational training. It becomes the task of the college, and more specifically the counselor, to assist the student in developing intellectual curiosity and in broadening his intellectual horizons.

Education cannot be forced onto people, but the college can stimulate a desire to be educated, by offering opportunities, choices, and a variety of experiences. The college must provide adequate facilities, teachers, and other resources for learning, and the counselor must assist in communicating the availability of these resources to the student. In addition, educational counseling must help the individual identify intellectual interests and life goals. In short, educational counseling must assist the student in gaining optimum advantage from his collegiate experience.

Vocational counseling. While higher education is designed to serve varied purposes, the expectations of many college students are to receive preparation for a specific vocation or, at the least, a background for such preparation. Unfortunately, the majority of students enter college ill-prepared to fulfill their expectations. Many enter with little understanding of the world of work and their future role in it. They are limited in the understanding of their capabilities and are hampered by their inability to project themselves into a vocational setting. This tends to reduce the efficiency of students in pursuing realistic goals; to give this direction is a major concern of vocational counseling. Although impossible to separate from either educational or personal-social counseling, student problems with emphasis on vocational decision-making account for another third of the counselor's efforts.

Vocational counseling and the related area of appraisal are directed toward assisting the individual to gain a clear understanding of himself, his abilities and limitations; his sources of motivation; and his needs, attitudes, and feelings. Individual appraisal, however, is only part of the task, and does not answer the common question, "What kind of a career should I consider?" Rapid technological change and shifting employment trends frequently present a picture too confusing for student comprehension. The counselor must aid the student in exploring the world of work and employment opportunities. Most counseling centers maintain extensive occupational information libraries. These contain information on worker qualifications and necessary training, and opportunities for individual expression, for advancement, or for individual need-satisfaction. Although no counselor is knowledgeable about all fields, he must be familiar with the broad occupational structure and with the sources of information available in specific areas of concern.

Personal-social counseling. The two previously discussed areas contain elements which could be classified as personal-social concerns. In counseling, however, this term is most frequently used to describe problems associated with an inadequacy in or a concern about an individual's adjustment to others—or his lack of acceptance of himself. While an educational institution is not intended to serve as a treatment center, nor a counselor as a therapeutic agent, both have a responsibility in helping students resolve minor adjustment difficulties. Problems such as "I can't seem to concentrate on my studies," "I have trouble getting along with my roommate," or "I lack self-confidence and get flustered before a class," may be eliminated or greatly reduced through skillful personal-social counseling. Although any of the techniques used in other types of counseling may be employed, the primary technique is that of the interview in which the student is encouraged to gain greater understanding of himself and his relationship to the problem situation.

Other Counseling Services

Faculty advising. Every student has occasion to be seen in a counseling relationship by a faculty member specifically qualified to assist in decisions concerning academic majors and courses of study. Academic counseling, perhaps more appropriately termed faculty advising, represents a general personal service which can be rendered by a wide variety of academicians with little specialized training in counseling. As a general rule, the majority of students have at least vague and tentative plans relative to their academic goals; they utilize faculty advisers as resource persons to supply information concerning specific course requirements, sequences, and prerequisites. The adviser needs to be aware of the general programs of the institution and, more specifically, the courses within his academic division. The skillful adviser will refer students to other specialists whenever the need arises. Most importantly, a good academic adviser must be a patient listener and a source of accurate information.

The role of the faculty member extends beyond program planning and academic advising. It is in the classroom and in private conferences that the faculty member comes to know the students, their needs and their problems. Although the professor is probably unable to engage in any intensive counseling relationship with individual students, his alertness to their needs and problems will enable him to refer them to proper specialists for further assistance. It is not surprising to see teachers become very interested in counseling, and many are of great assistance to students having a wide variety of problems.

Few academic specialists, however, are in a position to prepare themselves to be specialists in counseling. The counseling service, therefore, through the use of printed materials and short term in-service training meetings, can do much to promote sound faculty advising. The time spent in orienting faculty members to the basic principles of counseling is well worthwhile, since their cooperation is indispensable to the effective functioning of any counseling program. A faculty that is acquainted with the aims and objectives of a counseling program will be better prepared to identify and refer students needing assistance to the appropriate service.

Foreign student advising. Foreign student advising has become a specialty area within the division of student personnel, created to meet the needs of an increasing number of students from abroad. During the mid-60's some 80,000 foreign students from more than 140 different countries—nearly half from Asia or Africa—were enrolled in collegiate institutions of the United States. They were studying in about 1,800 institutions and nearly half were enrolled in engineering or agriculture. About half of the foreign students were enrolled in graduate study with the other half studying at the undergraduate level.

It is not only the number of foreign students but also the heterogeneity in personal backgrounds, cultural behavior, and educational preparation that causes concern for their adjustment to American institutions. These students are confronted with not only the usual problems of typical American students but also with those arising from adjustment to a strange environment. Just as Americans who go abroad are faced with the anxiety and frustration which comes from the loss of familiar signs guiding daily behavior, so too is the foreign student in this country. A tourist usually moves on quickly, and thus escapes the necessity of making an actual adjustment, but the foreign *student* must make some type of adjustment if he is to be effective in his study.

Personnel services in colleges and universities recognize the problems of adjustment facing the foreign student and reach out to provide assistance. In general, the foreign student adviser aims to assist the student in the process of admission, in developing English language proficiency, in orientation to both the college and the surrounding community, in academic planning, and in resolving personal problems through counseling. The task of the adviser is one of great proportions and he must solicit and coordinate the efforts of many members of the university community. His is a specialized role requiring a unique combination of knowledge of foreign cultures and skills in working with diverse problems. Foreign student advising is an essential aspect of the student personnel program and an integral part of the total educational program of any institution that accepts students from other countries.

Disciplinary counseling. During the past several decades considerable change has taken place in the concept of discipline on college campuses. Basically, the belief of discipline as a purely punitive measure has changed to that of discipline as a positive learning experience. This shift or modification of discipline has been slow in emerging, but is evidenced on many campuses today.

Rules and regulations on college campuses exist as a means of establishing an expected level of acceptable behavior and of protecting the rights of others. Infringement or violation of these rules and regulations requires some form of disciplinary action to bring about a change of behavior. Traditionally, disciplinary measures of a punitive nature have imposed penalties ranging from fines and restrictions to actual suspension or expulsion from the institution. While such punitive actions may have been justified for the protection of the university community, little of a positive corrective nature took place.

More recent approaches to disciplinary matters turn to counseling in order to help the offender learn from his experience and thereby modify his future behavior. The essence of this approach is well stated by E. G. Williamson:

> Discipline as organized student personnel work proceeds in an orderly fashion to help the individual search for an understanding of the causes of his misbehavior and for means of achieving his personality without continued disruptive and interfering expressions of his motivations.[8]

This type of discipline is not without complications. Effectiveness in the role of disciplinary counselor demands skill in working with students and a thorough knowledge of the regulations of the university. Specific attention must be given to protecting the rights of the individual student and to assuring equitable treatment.

While the process of administering discipline as a counseling and thus a learning experience is undoubtedly more cumbersome than meting out punishment, there can be little question of its ultimate success, for, in an institution devoted to the promotion of education, attention should be focused on the positive aspects of discipline.

Remedial services. Recognizing individual differences in educational preparation, many universities have introduced special programs to help students overcome their academic deficiencies. These remedial programs were particularly prevalent immediately after World War II, when many veterans were returning to school

---

[8] E. G. Williamson, *Student Personnel Services in Colleges and Universities* (New York: McGraw-Hill Book Company, 1961), p. 159.

after a considerable lapse in their educational progression. The provisions of the "G.I. Bill" allowed and encouraged many young men and women to seek admission to college. These new students, many of whom did not have a college preparatory background, needed help in this area. Quite common were remedial courses offered for credit in English and mathematics, as well as instruction in the development of sound study skills, speech, and reading habits. Many such courses are still offered on campuses, but very few institutions now give college credit for the development of the skills considered to be part of the student's pre-college preparation.

The placement of remedial services within the administrative structure varies, but, generally, the student personnel division is responsible. Other practices include the establishment of a separate clinic division, departmental assignment, or a coordinated effort of several departments. The demand for these remedial services has continued to be strong. The student who needs to develop reading, study or communication skills is being joined by many able students desiring to up-grade their skills in order to work more effectively.

Counseling plays a large part in the work done in these special clinic programs. Diagnostic techniques, best applied through individual counseling, are necessary to identify the source of learning difficulty, for the needs of the students vary so greatly that each situation may require a different starting point or problem-solving approach to help the student understand his problem. As a means of reducing the need for continuous individual instruction, programmed learning techniques are being used to permit the student to adjust or control his own learning rate. Special clinics can provide a valuable service to students who seek assistance in developing greater proficiency in the skills of learning.

Coordination of Services

The effectiveness of any counseling service depends upon the coordinated effort of the entire student personnel staff and the majority of the teaching faculty. Counseling services, as part of the total educational effort, have a responsibility to the faculty for providing information which will facilitate their work. Through the research efforts of counselors, studies are made of the characteristics of college students, their needs, and their goals. Counselors are available and should be utilized to interpret this information for their teaching colleagues. As good channels of communication are established, consultations regarding the progress or adjustment of individual students will follow. Through the exchange of information and the coordinated efforts of faculty and counselor, the educational objectives of the institution can best be served.

No single method of coordination will be equally effective on all campuses. The administrative organization and various line and staff relationships in the student personnel division, as well as within the total institution, will provide the framework upon which to build a coordinated service. Whatever this structure, the thinking and efforts of student groups, academic deans, administrators, faculty, and student personnel workers must create a system of coordinated counseling to meet student needs. Every segment of the institution must be made to feel responsible for contributing to the total education of its students.

Summary

Counseling is a process performed by the total faculty of a college as well as a function provided by specialists within the student personnel division. As a process, it is an integral aspect of the college's educational philosophy, which places the student and his unique constellation of abilities, interests, and needs at the heart of the educational endeavor. As a technical function, it consists of the skilled use of a wide variety of techniques and tools to supplement and aid the general service of the faculty.

As the college student's world becomes increasingly complex, the administrator of student services is continually challenged to stimulate and assist members of the faculty in discharging their counseling responsibilities. He must also provide for an organized counseling office, staffed with trained specialists, to provide the technical counseling services so urgently needed by young men and women as they meet their problems of maturation and education.

CHAPTER V

Health Services

Health services are usually responsible administratively to someone other than the dean of students. In most major colleges and universities, the administrative head of the health service holds a position parallel to that of the director of student personnel services and frequently reports directly to the president or a vice-president. The lines of administrative responsibility on smaller campuses frequently have this service as a subdivision of student personnel. Regardless of these line and staff relationships, its major concern is one of meeting students' needs, and thus it is a significant student personnel service.

As a part of the total education program of colleges and universities, health services enjoy a history of early acceptance. Amherst College has generally been credited with the development of the first student health program in 1861, and shortly thereafter numerous other Eastern schools initiated such programs. Early emphasis was on the physical condition of the student, with stress on physical education. College health services were concerned with reducing class absences due to health reasons; the prevention of epidemics; and the teaching of health education. With the development of inter- and intra-mural sports, however, they were forced to become involved in the physical welfare of participants.

During the early 1900's, infirmaries started to develop as part of the health services; the requirement of physical examinations for new students also came into existence. The importance of the mental health of college students was recognized and expressed about this time. The concept of student health has progressed from an early concern about physical conditioning, to limitation of student health services to the strictly medical aspects, to the modern concern for the total health of the college student. The present-day health service must embrace the positive aspects of education and prevention as well as the restorative measures.

Purposes

The primary reason for the existence of any health service in a college or university is the development of an adequate program for its students. This program extends beyond the medical aspects and includes a responsibility for the physical, emotional, and environmental health of the students. Its purposes are broad and varied in nature, but always include provision for dispensary and infirmary services, for the introduction of health education as part of the total education of students, and for the creation and maintenance of a healthful environment.

The requirements for an effective college health service were stated in a report to the Third National Conference on Health in Colleges and re-emphasized in the following Conference in 1954. These are:

1. Complete medical examination of each student upon entering college . . . ,
2. Individual conference between student and physicians, either directly following the entrance examination or shortly thereafter, to interpret the findings of the examination, to prepare the way for correction of abnormalities which have been disclosed, and to prescribe special programs for those found to be handicapped,
3. Arrangement of the student's academic and physical activity program in accordance with his best interests and through cooperation of college authorities and departments concerned with health activities,
4. Special medical examinations of students engaging in athletics and of special student groups,
5. Subsequent physical examinations which are deemed advisable because of the wishes of the student, the particular type of educational program in which he engages, the findings of previous examinations, or other information available to the health service,
6. Provision of medical care for emergency and ambulatory types of illness,
7. Consultation with specialists in various fields of medicine when desirable,
8. Hospitalization of students needing bed care,
9. Cooperation with other college departments in providing a healthful environment, including the execution of standard public health practices which are designed to eliminate or control communicable disease.[1]

The objectives of the college health service are completely com-

---

[1] *A Health Program for Colleges, A Report of the Third National Conference on Health in Colleges* (New York: National Tuberculosis Association, 1947), pp. 17–18.

patible with those of the student personnel program. Both are concerned with the total welfare of the student. Some functions of the health services, however, are areas of medical specialty while others have a direct relationship to some specific aspect of student personnel activity. Those areas involving a direct relationship will be discussed in the next few pages.

The Admissions Relationship

A very large percentage of colleges and universities have admission requirements concerning the health of the applicant; nearly all ask for a statement of the prospective student's physical condition. Practices vary considerably in regard to pre-admission physical examinations. With the great influx of students to campuses, this subject is currently under debate. At present, two practices dominate the scene: (A) students are required to have a physical examination at the time they enroll; or (B) students must present evidence of their health condition prior to the time they enroll in college. Typical of statements from schools which require a physical examination to be performed on campus as part of the admission policy is this one taken from the catalog of Miami University of Oxford, Ohio:

> Each student is given a physical and health examination when he enters the University by the staff of the Student Health Service and by members of the staffs of the departments of Physical and Health Education.
>
> The Health Service has been authorized by the Board of Trustees to require that all students be immune to smallpox and that they demonstrate by examination at the time of entrance and in subsequent regular examinations freedom from tuberculosis.[2]

The catalog of the University of Kentucky contains a statement reflecting the second general practice:

> The family physician of a student seeking to enter the University must complete and return a physical examination report on a form which the University will furnish the student after he makes application for admission.[3]

---

[2] *Miami University Catalogue for 1964–1965,* Series 62, No. 10 (Oxford, Ohio: December, 1963), p. 19.

[3] *Catalogue 1962–63, A Bulletin of the University of Kentucky,* LIV, No. 5 (Lexington, Kentucky: May, 1962), p. 17.

The arguments for and against either practice are numerous. Those favoring pre-admission physicals argue for the availability of the information at the time the student enrolls and for the advantages of not having to perform countless examinations in a short time. The burgeoning enrollments have added considerable support to this position. Physical examination at the time of enrollment has equal support. The arguments in favor of this practice cite the uniformity of information and records and the opportunity for special tests and examinations at the time the student is present.

Both practices have advantages and disadvantages which may be associated with the peculiarities of the college or university. Regardless of the approach involved, the basic objective remains constant—safe-guarding the student's health.

Class Attendance

Personnel services have an obvious interest in assuring optimum learning exposure through class attendance. Those students who repeatedly miss classes are either unaware of the objectives of the university and need counseling assistance, or are physically disabled and need the assistance of the health service. Both agencies have a responsibility in working with students in this area.

Many institutions expect students to attend classes and participate in examinations or else provide legitimate reasons for their irregularity. Some system of administering medical excuses must be developed to prevent abuses.

When there is evidence of physical disabilities suggesting the inadvisability of a student's participation in a class or activity, the physician has the responsibility of recommending a revision of the student's program. Such a revision should adhere to the general requirements and ingredients of the total college program and academic standards. Special privileges and concessions should not be granted merely to accommodate individual idiosyncrasies, but rather to serve legitimate health concerns. Special parking, choice of class hours and buildings, residence hall preferences, and library privileges should be recommended only in situations where compliance to the usual practice creates a hardship for the student.

Environmental Health Relationships

Environmental health factors impinge upon the entire educational program of the institution. The conditions of the classroom, housing facilities, food services, libraries, and gymnasiums are influences on the learning climate of the total college. The positive contributions of the best faculty can be reduced by poor lighting, poor ventilation, or poor housekeeping. A total health program must be concerned with the wide range of influences on the physical, mental, and social welfare of the student. The dean of students and the college health office have joint responsibilities for assuring favorable conditions.

Most colleges have a committee on environmental health, which should include representatives of the health service and the student personnel division. Its primary functions are to inform the college community of the importance of environmental health, to stimulate action to overcome deficiencies, and to promote effective health practices. The combined efforts of all college or university personnel must be directed toward providing an environment conducive to optimum learning.

Mental Health Responsibilities

Perhaps the most rapidly growing concern in the field of college health is that of mental health. The maturity and emotional growth of the student are recognized as part of his total education. In providing for the mental health needs of college students, the student personnel division and the health service have mutual responsibilities. This mutuality of concern implies some similarity of function and demands effective communication to insure a coordinated effort in maintaining the best service for students.

The mental health problems of a college community are not different, in kind, from those which might arise in any community; however, the uniqueness of a college population tends to produce difficulties in proportions not usually found in other segments of the general society. Here, young adults are searching for meaning and self-identity. Furthermore, the period of late adolescence, characteristic of the college student, is one of continuous adjustment pressures and problems. These pressures, coupled with the need for academic achievement, frequently produce emotional disturbances varying in severity.

Dana L. Farnsworth, long recognized as a pioneer and leader in the development of college health services, expresses the magnitude of the problem in the following statement:

> Those who work in the field of student health are by now well aware of the statistics indicating that, by conservative estimate, at least 10 per cent of college students experience sufficient emotional conflict to warrant professional treatment and that, during their period of residence in the college community, 18-25 per cent of students will seek consultation with a psychiatrist if this service is available. (Two-thirds of these come on their own initiative, one-third by referral.)[4]

Present day mental health services in college range from the provision of a complete psychiatric service with a staff of psychiatrists, clinical psychologists, social workers, and nurses, to a total lack of provision in this area. Large universities provide their own psychiatric services, while many other colleges utilize professional consultants from within the community. The range of services provided must necessarily vary with the personnel of the health service. Farnsworth recognizes staffing problems, but states that an adequately staffed service should be concerned with the following activities: (A) diagnostic interviews, (B) referral to appropriate community resources, (C) short-term therapy, (D) emergency treatment and crisis consultation with any of the individuals involved in helping the student, (E) consultation with university personnel, (F) representing the community in a protective capacity, and (G) teaching, formally and informally.[5]

In conjunction with the usual student personnel functions, the psychiatric service can provide a valuable evaluation service. Counselors and other personnel workers are frequently confronted with the question of whether a student is of sufficient emotional stability to profit from the usual personnel services or whether he needs professional psychiatric assistance. Expert medical consultation can be of great value in determining the disposition of such problem cases.

---

[4] Dana L. Farnsworth, *College Health Services in the United States* (Washington, D.C.: American College Personnel Association, 1965), p. 21.

[5] *Ibid.*, pp. 22–24.

Colleges and universities are educational institutions and should not attempt to become therapeutic centers. If a student is sufficiently disturbed that he needs extensive psychotherapy, referral should be made to an appropriate agency. However, short-term therapy, ranging up to five or six visits, often proves beneficial in providing the assistance necessary for the student to continue with his educational pursuits. Demands of students for service, the objectives of the institution, and the critically short supply of qualified psychiatrists are some of the reasons for limiting therapy.

Student Insurance Plans

Student health services are designed to provide medical care to students and it seems appropriate that the recipients of such service be responsible for its support. Most colleges and universities finance the health service, at least in part, through student fees. Routine medical service is then provided without cost to the student, but all types of medical assistance cannot be offered on a cost-free basis. Extensive medical care and hospitalization must be provided through some system of insurance.

Insurance plans are used by many of the student groups of colleges and universities. These student health insurance plans, as the name implies, are for the benefit of the students, and student groups should be involved in the determination of the plan to be utilized. It is, therefore, the responsibility of the student personnel division to promote student investigation of the problems and alternatives in providing health insurance, and the responsibility of the health service to offer sound medical advice concerning the suitability of alternate plans. Representatives of the various commercial insurance agencies should meet with student groups and university officials to determine the various types of coverage available and the costs of such programs. Numerous plans are in existence and several appear to be satisfactory. The suitability of any student health plan is dependent upon the peculiar characteristics of the student body of the institution, the nature of coverage required, and the services offered by the health service. Therefore, careful consideration must be given before determining which insurance will be most appropriate.

Summary

It is clear that health programs contribute to the total education of the college student. The range of specific services rendered varies according to the resources and facilities of the institution. Numerous objectives of a health program parallel those of the student personnel program and require a coordinated effort in realizing maximum implementation. Continuous attention must be directed to providing a healthful environment conducive to learning; a health service for ministering to the needs of students; and a health education program to develop positive, long-lasting health attitudes and practices.

CHAPTER VI

Student Housing

Student housing is recognized as an integral aspect of the total educational program. As emphasized previously, effective education on the campus depends greatly upon the degree to which the total environment provides a consistent, forceful stimulus to intellectual growth.

Residence halls are, therefore, no longer thought of as merely a place for students to eat and sleep while they are being educated in the classroom. Rather they are increasingly viewed as integral aspects of the college's educational program which requires an integration of the living unit and its physical facilities with the academic offerings and intellectual spirit of the institution.

Housing Under Scrutiny

Many social trends are forcing critical attention upon even the most traditional educational practices. Waves of new students, greater pressure for higher academic standards, expanded budgets, the incredible growth of scientific and technological knowledge, the application of research in the behavioral sciences and educational processes, and the rapidly enlarging role of universities in world affairs, are merely a few of the forces contributing to the need for conscientious evaluation of existing practices and for a greater effort to increase educational effectiveness and economy.

Student housing is one aspect of higher education being subjected to intensive study. The enormous investment of capital and administrative energy to provide current and future student housing justifies such evaluation. The challenge to do a better job educationally further illustrates the need for critical examination and fruitful development. Questions about the effective role of student housing are being asked by a public which has the right to demand quality with quantity in American higher education. Student personnel workers are among those who must provide the answers.

The expansion of residence halls made it possible to house more students and thus take care of the increase in college enrollment during the years following World War II. The lack of recognition of the contribution that residence halls make toward educational development, however, has kept the quality of this effort back. Those responsible for the erection of the impressive number of new residence halls have not integrated their construction and purpose with the basic educational program of the colleges. Yet, even a cursory review of research, experimentation, and new programming reveals that residence halls have tremendous unrealized potential for enriching students' educational experience—through activities, student relationships, and sub-cultures.

Objectives of the Residence Hall Program

Mueller surveyed current housing objectives and found the objectives were for physical accommodation, promotion of academic learning, personal development, public relations, and control of student conduct. An objective that should be added to this list is that of individualizing relations with the student through the residence hall system. The objectives of residence halls are to a large degree the objectives of the over-all student personnel program. This is as it should be because it is the living situation that makes the greatest impact upon the individual student. Mueller further observed that the objective of promoting academic learning, which was the one most closely related to the primary institutional goal, existed only in the chance, informal, cross-fertilization of ideas through student discussions.[1]

Such informal methods are inadequate to meet current demands for an increased "impact of college," to use Freedman's term.[2] Objectives must be clarified in order to place primary emphasis upon those concerns which should be dominant. These include emphasis upon faculty-student contacts outside the classroom; intellectually and academically oriented activities; as well as programs, libraries, seminar rooms, and other physical facilities designed to make

---

[1] Kate Hevner Mueller, *Student Personnel Work in Higher Education* (Boston: Houghton Mifflin Company, 1961), p. 175.

[2] Mervin B. Freedman, *Impact of College, New Dimensions in Higher Education* (Washington, D.C.: U.S. Department of Health, Education and Welfare, 1960).

learning and intellectual activity facts of every day life for resident students.

In order to accomplish the foregoing objectives, a staff which has been selected and trained to carry them out is essential. Tasks of secondary importance such as student control, recreational and social activities, and other routine procedures should not be permitted to absorb its time and energy. The reformulation of educational objectives of residence hall living and the development of programs to achieve such objectives is a much more difficult, fundamental, and far-reaching task than merely reverbalizing high sounding phrases. Involved is changing the attitudes and perceptions of nearly every person employed by the college.

The pervasive nature of the educational role of residence hall living requires cooperation by the total campus community—student leaders, parents, counselors, admissions officers, faculty members, business and alumni office staff members, and maintenance personnel. Because the operation of residence halls involves an unusually wide variety of specialized and often partisan interests, the varied perceptions of a good residence hall must be considered in establishing policies and programs.

Another influence complicating the construction of a positive, educational role for residence halls is the resident student body itself. Many students see group housing and its activities as an escape from the rigorous, intellectual life of the university. The thrill of learning and the satisfying sense of achievement must be made meaningful in the lives of many students, if they are to accept willingly and participate eagerly in an educationally sound residence hall program.

A third complicating factor is the lack of examples, both actual buildings and administrative organizations, which meet the diverse conditions existing in various colleges and universities. Institutional needs vary almost as much as individual needs. Therefore, it is of utmost importance that each college develop its own housing program, and not attempt to copy one that is successful in a different situation.

To meet the wide range of student preferences and needs most campuses must provide a variety of housing facilities ranging from low cost with minimal facilities to higher cost, luxury types; from small buildings to large complexes; and from "cooperatives" to privately built and operated halls. Administrators concerned with residence halls must eliminate confusion regarding their educational roles. Further, they must be well enough informed to interpret to their colleagues the relative advantages and disadvantages of various types of buildings and programs.

Selecting and Training Residence Hall Staff

Colleges have provided for necessary supervision and educational leadership in their residence halls in a variety of ways. Some have used housemothers. Others have used undergraduate or graduate student assistants. Still others have used faculty members or professionally-trained student personnel workers. Regardless of the method used to staff the halls, the quality of the people is second in importance only to the basic institutional philosophy of the role residence halls play in the total educational program. Increasing recognition of the importance of residence halls and their rapidly expanding systems requires that there be more and better trained staff members. It is imperative that student personnel administrators give creative attention to the most effective and economical methods of staffing residence halls to achieve their educational objectives.

Traditionally, the duties of staff members in residence halls involved maintenance of a modicum of order, protection of buildings and equipment, and prevention of improper behavior. The modern concept, however, has broadened to include major emphasis upon the educational benefits—student government, honor systems, closer faculty relations, integration with academic activities, and housing grouped according to special educational and vocational interests. Unfortunately, job perceptions and descriptions have not changed and the consequences in all too many cases have been friction among staff members and students alike.

Even when the philosophy of residence hall programming has been clearly defined, the difficulty of recruiting an adequate number of qualified applicants has often determined staff roles. Most institutions are having a problem maintaining their traditional staffing patterns, because of a shortage of applicants for residence hall positions. As a rule, mature women have been recruited to serve as housemothers for both men's and women's residence halls and represent a staff source worthy of development. At present, other employment opportunities, extended coverage of social security, and increased demands upon staff members make it more and more difficult to locate qualified applicants among this group. Those institutions which have been able to recruit older women have found them to be effective, if given training.

The use of undergraduates in this capacity poses a number of problems. Such factors as the lure of apartment living, requirement of student-teaching away from campus, the desire for greater freedom than a resident assistantship permits, financial grants and job opportunities in academic departments, all tend to discourage applicants from this group. Consequently, many colleges using this system have started using juniors or even sophomores to staff their halls. As a result, student government in the halls oftentimes suffers from lack of competent leadership.

Despite problems associated with staffing halls with undergraduate assistants, their use may well be expanded in the future because of their availability—particularly in institutions without graduate divisions. The fact that their use underscores the educational objectives of self-responsibility, self-discipline, and self-government must also be considered.

Most of the larger institutions have traditionally used graduate students as resident assistants. Residence hall experience is a valuable supplement to the training of future college teachers, as well as an excellent experience for graduate students in many disciplines. However, an increasingly greater problem is developing for the hall director in recruiting staff members here, despite the rapidly growing number of graduate students. Competition from the higher stipends given for fellowships and assistantships in academic departments, greater demand to have graduate students serve as teachers, more stringent and time-consuming scholastic requirements, and the increased turnover caused by field requirements, marriage, and student mobility make it imperative for the student personnel administrator to develop positions which are compatible with successful graduate work. He must have a well-planned program which benefits the graduate assistant through personal and professional growth, and must maintain continuous communication with graduate departments about openings and the value of residence hall experience to the future professional careers of graduates in a great variety of fields.

Many student personnel administrators feel that staffing problems would be solved if they could have a complete residence hall staff of professionally trained student personnel workers. Unfortunately, even with adequate funds to pay the increasingly higher salaries such persons can demand, there are still a number of major problems which tax the skill of the most competent staff director. The availability of other personnel positions and the extreme limitations on personal freedom cause frequent turnover. Differing points of view, abrupt changes in policies due to turnover, and friction in staff relations because of inter-related job assignments, all become more intense and disruptive within a staff of trained persons. To secure the advantages of training and experience it is imperative that the organizational and administrative structure of the hall system specifically provide for continued professional growth. Personnel must be integrated into the total institutional student personnel staff, become involved in policy formation, and participate in resolving campus problems.

The use of faculty members to staff residence halls offers solutions to a number of problems related to the integration of residence hall living with the total educational program of the college. However, it may not resolve other problems associated with their day-to-day operation. The faculty member has a primary obligation to his teaching, research, publication, and related duties. He often views his residence hall work as an added duty, an interference, or practically a voluntary contribution to the college. These views make it difficult for non-academic personnel to supervise the faculty member in the performance of his residence hall duties. Certain circumstances, nevertheless, indicate that student personnel administrators would do well to recruit and train faculty members for residence halls positions, rather than to patch up one of the traditional plans. They must consider the increasing number of faculty members who have had experience in residence hall work.

Regardless of the specific plan or combination of plans used to staff the residence halls, there are certain procedures which should be followed:

1. The institution should have a clear statement of the contribution residence halls are expected to make toward the achievement of its educational objectives. Preferably such a statement should come from an all-college committee representing the gov-

erning board, top administrators, faculty, student personnel workers, and the student body.

2. There should be job descriptions for staff members containing not only the usual list of duties and functions but also emphasizing the relationship of positions to one another and to various aspects of the total institution. Such descriptions should give more attention to cooperative effort, educational expectations, and should exemplify institutional values and ideals rather than merely stating mundane duties. For effective staff relations and individual performances it is important that prospective staff members have the clearest possible picture of their jobs and an understanding of the criteria which will be applied in evaluation of their work.

3. There should be a clearly stated expectancy for continued professional growth on the job. Such a statement should be supported by a carefully conceived in-service training program which contributes to objectivity, to intellectual curiosity, and to an educational relationship with hall residents.

4. Job interviews should be frank, realistic, and positive. Misunderstandings or even false information undermine job morale and staff effort with friction, reduced efficiency and increased personnel turnover. Honest discussion of impending problems, probable areas of disagreement, policy conflicts, special duty assignments, and imminent personnel changes can, on the other hand, lead to objectivity, harmony, morale, and cooperative effort. In addition, information about the educational role of the halls, institutional provisions and hopes for continued professional growth, plus evident respect for the contributions of all staff members, contribute to the success of an interview and enable prospective staff members and the interviewer to evaluate each other.

5. High staff morale, efficiency, and enthusiasm are not characteristic of situations where there are no irritations, differences of opinion, or needed changes. Rather, they develop from open discussion and resolution of difficulties by established procedures and sound working relationships. Students have the ability to very rapidly detect friction, disinterest, and hypocrisy. Consequently, the intimate residence hall community poses a difficult challenge to establish the most productive and satisfying climate through development of healthy, active relationships.

Residence Hall Programming

Programming embraces broad areas of activities—meetings, effective use of facilities, student involvement, and staff presence which characterize a residence hall. Unfortunately, many college staff members perceive hall programming in its social or recreational aspects, and thus have a narrow, negative view of the positive educational values that can be achieved through these halls. Libraries, receptions for visiting personalities, faculty-led seminars on current topics of interest, appointment of faculty members having a continuing relationship with each living unit, and the development of student government, all are significant aspects of a good residence hall program.

More important than even the finest programming is student involvement. Sound educational programs cannot be imposed upon a group of students. To be effective, such programs must be participated in by students who earnestly desire such activities. To accomplish this requires imaginative planning and capable staff members. Similarly, the support of the faculty and college administration must be secured if the educational emphasis in the residence halls is to be representative of the institution. Support for student government in the residence halls must also reflect an institutional commitment to the participation of students in the basic affairs of the college. Institutional concern for the intellectual growth of students is most easily reflected when daily relationships indicate that residence halls are basic to the college and not merely a necessary—but peripheral—adjunct.

An important objective of the hall program is the establishment of identity between the residence hall and the total institution. Such identity arises from traditions, activities, self-perception, and involvement of residents of one hall with those in other housing units on campus.

Fraternities and Sororities as Integral Aspects of the Residence Program

On many college campuses, fraternities and sororities represent an untapped resource in the residence program. Too often they have been viewed as mere social organizations, rather than as integral parts of the institution's academic efforts. In such instances, the attention that fraternal groups receive is oriented towards controlling their social and recreational activities in an effort to prevent interference with scholastic achievement or to inhibit misconduct. This view of fraternities has limited the attempts of student personnel workers to broaden the members' perception of their group's educational goal. Such broadening is the first step toward bringing fraternities into the educational mainstream. This task may be achieved in a manner similar to that for residence halls; namely, by adopting a carefully constructed statement of policy for an educational role; by providing adequate staff to assist in positive programming; and by integrating the efforts of all aspects of the community including faculty members and alumni leaders.

The idealistic basis for fraternities, combined with their *esprit de corps* and tradition of self-government, all provide excellent starting points for achieving the highest objectives of the institution of which they are a part. Failure to capitalize on these assets indicates institutional prejudice, ignorance, and indifference which reflect unfavorably upon the institution and cast doubt upon its conception of itself as a totality.

Meeting the Needs of Off-Campus Students

Commuting students living at home and in private rooming houses present a special challenge to the student personnel worker. Because of day-to-day concern with residence halls and fraternal units, staff time and energy is almost totally consumed in this area to the exclusion of any creative thinking and planning for students not in group housing. It is not surprising, then, when such students form their own groups, their own campus sub-cultures, their own identities and status-giving norms. Special lunch rooms in the student union and periodic social or recreational activities are not sufficient inspiration for any real involvement in campus affairs. In fact, it is possible that a preponderance of specialized activities may serve to further remove their interests from total campus involvement, separating rather than integrating the student body.

This problem is often erroneously labelled lack of communication. While this may be a contributing factor, in reality it is one of assimilating off-campus students into the mainstream of the campus. It is important to offer these students some of the benefits attainable through group living. A procedure followed on some campuses has been the assignment of all non-resident students to halls as associate members, with privileges including participation in activities. Such affiliation offers the non-resident student a group with which he can identify and a place to meet and make friends. He has an opportunity to meet faculty members and college officials and often a place to dine with other students.

A second procedure used on many campuses involves special programming, sponsored by the union or student government in the student union building. Group commitment and the personal touch are keys to the success of this program. An organization is necessary to recruit hosts and hostesses and to invite guest participants—students and others. Conversations and associations should be followed by positive suggestions for participation in other campus events. Rather than restricting its membership to those ostensibly being served, such a project's members should reflect campus-wide participation and enthusiasm. For this reason, such a project should attempt to secure cooperation and support from departmental clubs, special interest groups, and campus service organizations.

A third method of actively involving the off-campus student in campus affairs has been the formation of a precinct or district organization. Each area has one or more representative on a central governing committee. The success of such an organization depends largely upon the extent of staff investment in it, the provision for continuity, the feeling among participants that the institution recognizes their influence, and the enlistment of support from all agencies within the university community.

Current Trends, Problems, and Issues

Any discussion of trends, problems, and issues regarding student housing also implies one of general educational directions. Certain aspects of these issues, a few of which are outlined here, are directly related to the basic objectives of housing.

1. *Racial and other forms of discrimination.* Racial discrimination in college and university housing is rapidly being eliminated by various governmental provisions and by a growing realization that discrimination is inconsistent with sound educational practice.

The student personnel administrator is often in a dilemma when some parents and, less frequently, students demand immediate roommate changes because of racial differences. From the student personnel point of view, roommate compatibility is a significant factor in college success. But frequent changes in housing assignments because of differences in race, religion, or national origin serve to perpetuate the practices that are being terminated by institutional non-discriminatory policies. It is important that these policies be made clear in housing, literature, orientation sessions, and new student meetings. All staff members should be thoroughly informed, and no changes requested by parent or student based on discrimination should be approved until every effort has been made by the student to adapt. Changes made after an adjustment period of three to five weeks should be made only on the basis of incompatibility, illness, or emotional distress, as in non-discriminatory situations. An institutional policy of eliminating discrimination is a general educational practice which is being increasingly accepted by the public. The policy should be clearly enunciated and implemented wholeheartedly by all staff members.

2. *Co-educational housing.* In most cases, a student body does not grow by so many men or so many women a year. Consequently, the need to expand housing in relation to changing needs has resulted in clusters of halls, some for men and some for women, with central dining facilities. The educational advantages of co-ed dining have long been recognized, particularly by smaller institutions. Some hall complexes include high-rise buildings, housing men on some floors and women on others, with central lounge, dining, and other facilities. Regardless of the motivation for such trends, common facilities make significant contributions to the hall educational program, improve decorum in the dining halls, and increase stability and continuity in the governmental structure of the hall. Aside from these advantages, such excesses as panty raids and other similar disorders are reduced. Student personnel workers need to be alert if they are to utilize the strengths of these facilities. Full participation in planning sessions and creative programming will bring about the greatest benefits for such housing.[3]

---

[3] See Elizabeth A. Greenleaf, "Co-educational Residence Halls: An Evaluation," *Journal of the National Association of Women Deans and Counselors,* XXV, No. 3 (1962), 106–111.

3. *Environmental control.* There is probably no issue causing greater student and staff unrest and frustration than that of dress and behavior regulations. Increasingly students feel that these matters are best left to their own discretion, and that it is not the prerogative of the administration to interfere. In turn, college administrators receive complaints, through residence hall personnel, from parents, faculty, and students about standards regarding dress and behavior. Perhaps discord between students and authority is inevitable; nevertheless, it creates unrest, wastes time and energy, lowers morale, and detracts from educational achievement. While an entire book would not be able to cover the issues and possible solutions, good practice does include the following:

(a.) Students, faculty, and administration should all be involved in the establishment of standards, resolution of differences, and adjudication of infractions, depending on the level and degree of seriousness,

(b.) At a primary level, students should have a large part in suggesting standards, establishing operating rules, and handling violations,

(c.) Expectancies should be continually and carefully communicated through all available channels such as literature, student newspaper, student government, speeches, orientation, and leadership training sessions. Vaguely communicated expectancies or hypocritical statements only aggravate issues and make their resolution more difficult,

(d.) Emotionally tinged phrases such as *in loco parentis* or student rights, and vague meaningless concepts such as appropriate dress or exemplary behavior, need to be replaced with well defined terms. Issues based on emotion and ambiguity tend to embroil large numbers of students without clarifying what the differences are and how they can be resolved,

(e.) Clear channels for the presentation of differing points of view, submission of suggestions and exchange of ideas are essential elements of any democratic situation. The staff role in most conflicts is to keep such channels open rather than to permit repression of discussion.

4. *Cost reduction.* Pressure for reducing costs in the various types of housing is great and will increase in the future. Usually this pressure is directed against those "extras" or "frills," such as

educational activities, libraries, study facilities, counseling, and guest programs. Often these programs are most significant to the education of the student—the object of all expenditures.

Students need to appreciate and understand the financing of their facilities, just as they need to be a party to their own education. Once informed regarding costs, they will vigorously support the institution in its efforts. Thus it is important to include a frank and complete statement regarding costs at meetings of parents, new students, alumni, and high school representatives.

Frequently, students will reject cost reduction plans under which they do some of their own housecleaning, kitchen work, or reception service; yet at the same time complain of high costs. Similarly, some students will move from cheaper university housing to private apartments or fraternities at a much higher cost to them. Thus, it is obvious that independence, group morale, and peer relationship are closely interrelated factors in housing satisfaction. It is particularly important that the student personnel administrator receive feedback through student government and other channels regarding costs and student reaction to facilities, programming, and conveniences.

5. *Relative advantages and disadvantages of various types of housing.* Most institutions feel they should provide a variety of housing types to meet the needs and satisfy the desires of a heterogeneous student body. The student personnel worker needs more information regarding the educational advantages and disadvantages of all types of housing. Certain questions need immediate research: What students profit most from a group situation compared to those living in private homes? What is the effect of moving frequently from one residence to another? How does paternalism to varying degrees help or hinder self-government, self-discipline, and self-direction?

One of the effects of the current trend against supervision of students' out-of-class life has been to encourage the older student to move out of group housing. Such a trend often leaves the residence hall and fraternity without the mature leadership of upper-classmen upon whom most programs depend for success. Traditionally, the rewards in status and experience had been sufficient to attract and keep most upper-classmen in group housing. If these rewards are not now sufficient, what should replace them?

There are a variety of topics which need to be researched and explained. The student personnel administrator must be among the leaders in stimulating such research, not among the crowd bemoaning changing times and values.

6. *Planning housing facilities.* The process of planning new housing should be representative of the entire institution. All too often planning has been done by architects, in consultation with business offices, who have little regard for the educational objectives of housing. Unfortunately, just as often, the student personnel staff and faculty members, who might have had something to contribute to the planning process, have stood by waiting to be asked instead of providing guide lines, suggestions, lists of needed facilities, and observations. Planning should be a continuous, positive process. It should not be a one-time negative event, consisting of finding out what was wrong in the last building and correcting it in the next. The student personnel staff is obligated to collect and present suggestions for the improvement of all physical facilities. These suggestions should include discussions about the optimum size of buildings and plans for effective physical arrangements bringing about natural groupings. A final responsibility of the student personnel worker is to lead the institution in formulating an operational philosophy regarding the role of residence living.

Summary

This chapter has described the significant role which the resident unit can play in the institution's educational program. It has emphasized the importance of having an institutional philosophy, the need for careful staff recruitment and training, and the necessity for integrating the efforts of faculty as well as other staff members in initiating and furthering a truly educational program. It has emphasized the necessity to have students involved and activities planned in order to have an effective residence program. Lastly, it emphasized that the student personnel administrator and his staff must play a leading role in showing college administration that the residence unit is a significant educational aspect of the college.

CHAPTER VII

Student Activities

Only in the United States is there so much emphasis on student life outside the classroom. One needs only to skim the popular magazines and newspapers of recent years to realize that what our collegians are doing is of great popular interest. Unfortunately for American higher education, the news from college campuses has all too often been confined to student activities. Demonstrations and "teach-ins" in the immediate past have overshadowed the traditional news of athletics, social events, and misbehavior. Sensational news from either extreme is a poor vehicle for transmitting the real value and nature of student activities on the college campus, and for making progress toward changing public and campus concepts of the purpose and potentiality of activities. Good or bad, campus life is currently undergoing a scrutiny which it has traditionally escaped. Advances in behavioral research and application to the campus scene of techniques from a number of the behavioral sciences, are yielding findings which undergird the efforts of student personnel workers to develop the quality of extra-curricular life to a point where it truly complements and supplements formal education.[1]

Objectives of Student Activities

Student activities encompass such a wide range of interests, content, and program that it is probably improper to speak of them as an entity. As emphasized in Chapter I, a student's out-of-class life bears directly on what he learns, becomes, and achieves in college. Therefore, student personnel workers, as the staff members to whom responsibility is delegated for this area have a professional obliga-

[1] The term "extra-curricular" has never been completely satisfactory, although in wide use. "Student activities" and "co-curricular" are probably more descriptive but not fully accepted in use. Similarly, "the third curriculum" proposed by some writers to distinguish extra-class activities from the required curriculum and the elective curriculum has not been widely accepted. *See* Robert W. Frederick, *The Third Curriculum* (New York: Appleton-Century-Crofts, Inc., 1959).

tion to apply the same standards and attention to student activities that a classroom professor has to apply to his class work. The scope of experiences and the ephemeral nature of out-of-class life make the implementation of the concept difficult and often debatable. Some students and faculty alike reject the idea that a student's private life is a proper matter of concern for university officials.

Because of the ambiguity of the term "student activities," and the difficulty in changing the traditional perceptions of activities from social and recreational emphases to an academic and intellectual orientation, attempts to postulate specific lists of objectives duplicate those of the objectives of education itself. Ideas frequently mentioned are: attaining a balanced personality; increasing breadth of interests; developing human relations skills; exercising responsibility and judgment; participating in self-government; and developing loyalty to the college.

Mueller classified into four categories the contributions which student activities might be expected to make to a student's development: those

> "complementing classroom instruction or enhancing academic learning; developing social-interaction; providing for a profitable use of leisure time; and encouraging better values and higher standards."[2]

A fifth general category of contributions is composed of those activities which facilitate and encourage the student's participation as a responsible citizen in local, national, and international affairs. Any one activity may well make a number of contributions; thus, such a classification serves primarily as a basis for discussing various types of activities from the point of view of the student personnel worker and administrator.

Representative of activities complementing and supplementing academic learning are departmental clubs such as are sponsored by the music, language, theater, speech, government, business, science, and education departments or schools. Frequently publications are an official or traditional part of the journalism or English departments. The art department on many campuses has an active out-of-class organization which promotes art displays, holds lectures, and stimulates all-campus interest in art. Experience in the activ-

[2] Kate Hevner Mueller, *Student Personnel Work in Higher Education* (Boston: Houghton Mifflin Company, 1961), p. 275.

ities of groups related to an academic area can make learning come alive and be more than an academic exercise to the students involved. But it would be short-sighted to assume that all activities should stem from the academic departments, or that only students studying in a particular department could or should participate in activities related to that department.

Representative of activities which contribute to social interaction include many of the program areas of the student union; traditional all-campus events such as Homecoming, Senior Week, Mothers' Day, and Alumni Day; the big but fast disappearing social events such as the Junior Prom, Military Ball, and similar occasions; recognition societies and government groups; and even religious and service organizations. Despite the trend to disparage such activities, the contributions they make are significant and necessary. If all were abolished on any given day on a campus, the students would begin to organize new ones the next day. Whether from an innate or culturally derived need, a student needs experience working with his peers in order to learn who he is, what he can do, and how to achieve his wants. Overemphasis on social activities in the past and the intense climate of many campuses at present have caused the social area to fall into disrepute in educational circles. Student problems arising from confusion, alienation from tradition, and conflicts regarding values and goals serve to emphasize the importance of socialization in the maturation and education of young people. Thus, from the personnel point of view, the socialization process, which was traditionally carried forward by the relatively isolated, ethnocentric campus, must be identified and re-established through currently acceptable activities if they are to contribute to the total growth of today's youth.

It is difficult to name activities which contribute to the profitable use of leisure time without appearing to cast doubt upon their worth. Faculty, parents, and students alike would probably cry, "What leisure time?" The pressures of academic life, either actual or imagined, are growing so intense that the need to consider the wise and profitable use of leisure is academic. The need for recreation, however, is genuine, and the value to efficient functioning is great. Students have leisure and will use it in some way. Intramural sports in which they participate, intercollegiate sports which they watch, hiking, dancing, card-playing, or volunteer social service work, all represent diverting, re-creating activities which, when properly balanced, can make students better students and better people. What is one person's poison may be another's cup of tea, so the offerings need to be diverse, convenient, attractive, and relatively inexpensive. Mueller summarizes the point of view succinctly by commenting,

> These programs may seem superficial and unacademic, but they actually have a strong therapeutic value, not only because they absorb the energies and high spirits in harmless, if not actually profitable, avenues but also because they build morale and cause divergent personalities to coalesce and build an *esprit de corps* which invests the collegiate way of life with its strongest emotional and spiritual values.[3]

The formation of attitudes, values, and standards is a constant process evolving out of one's daily experience. Therefore, the activities program, synthesizing as it does the entire impact of college, is in a particularly strategic position to facilitate the formation of those attitudes, values, and standards, which the college by its words and precepts, feels its students should possess. Eddy summarizes the effect of the total environment by concluding that

> An all too common conception of a college education is that it includes only the narrowly defined academic process involving just the teacher and the student. Many college graduates agree, however, that their education took place as much outside the classroom as within its narrow walls, and was as much a result of all that surrounded them as of the formal lecture and seminar. Some refer to this larger, encompassing classroom as "the climate of the campus." We call it the environment. But, no matter what term is used, we identify it as a factor of paramount significance in the development of character.[4]

Thus, from the student personnel point of view, the student learns and becomes what he experiences; and therefore the quality, standards, and nature of student activities are a concern of the entire institution. Further, from an educational point of view, slipshod procedures, unethical practices, selfish interests, or superficiality cannot be permitted to characterize student activities any more than they could be permitted to characterize classroom matters.

---

[3] *Ibid.*, p. 279.

[4] Edward D. Eddy, Jr., *The College Influence on Student Character* (Washington, D.C.: American Council on Education, 1959), pp. 132–133.

There is the point of view exemplified by the plaintive comment of a student quoted by Eddy, "Why don't they let us alone? I like this fraternity because it's the one place on campus where I can really be myself;"[5] nevertheless, the proper educational goal is to strive to raise standards and values through all student experiences.

The role of student activities in encouraging and facilitating students' interest and participation in local, national, and international affairs is a relatively new emphasis on most college campuses, in most cases since World War II. As early as 1947 the President's Commission on Higher Education observed that

> As a rule the graduates of our schools and colleges have not been adequately prepared for the tasks of citizenship and have been apathetic about performing them . . . Many of them were not only uninformed about national and world problems but were markedly reluctant to take part in social enterprises at any cost to themselves . . .
>
> We dare not let this state of affairs continue. Every resource of education must be mobilized and focused on the task of establishing in students a habit of social action enlightened by insight into the responsibilities of citizenship at all levels—local, national and international.[6]

Unfortunately, the American college campus until recently has all too often served as a cloister, protecting young people from disturbing thoughts; as the stage for superficial busy-work, turning out "well-rounded leaders;" or as a retreat to fancied security for young people not ready, either by motivation or maturity, for the chaotic, conflicting, often shocking nature of the modern world. Often, the alumni of these years are now those who question the validity of concerns by university students with such problems as nuclear testing, foreign policy, disarmament, race relations, ethics in government and business, and political party traditions. Students the world over are showing greater interest in national and international affairs and are becoming more overt and aggressive in expressing their views. Students in the United States with their freedom of information, inquiry, speech, and assembly must not fail to keep pace.

It is not just the right of students but their obligation as favored citizens in a rich society to study issues carefully, to form opinions

---

[5] *Ibid.*, p. 135.

[6] *Higher Education for American Democracy*, Vol. I, *Establishing the Goals* (Washington, D.C.: U.S.G.P.O., 1947), p. 51.

regarding them, and to express their views competently. A function of the student activities program is to encourage and facilitate this aspect of education within the context of the college. It is a cliché to note that the campus should be a laboratory of democracy. Real significance lies in the further observations that campus experiences of a student determine, to a large extent, his understanding and perceptions of the values for which the institution stands. Campus life reflects institutional values more than verbalized statements.

A critical frontier for the student personnel worker, as far as student activities are concerned, is altering the common perception of them and making them truly significant in the lives of their participants. To bring about this change, he must first transform the concept he has of his role as a maintainer of the *status quo,* the keeper of morals, or the judge of all virtue, to that of an educator in the broadest sense. Then, and only then, will he be able to lead his institution to a new stance on faculty participation in student activities, integration of extra-class life with the academic objectives of the institution, and adoption of policies encouraging exploration and inquiry rather than conformity and superficiality.

The Role of the Faculty Adviser

A key element in the integration of student activities with the academic and intellectual objectives of the college is the faculty member serving as adviser to the organization or activity concerned. The contribution which he makes depends upon a wide variety of factors. Unfortunately, the influence of tradition may be strongly negative, because all too often faculty advisers have served in name only, signing documents and occasionally attending an installation banquet. Indeed, some faculty members rationalize such a position, of being available for advice when needed but otherwise keeping out of the affairs of the club, as being educationally sound. If the objectives of the activity had no educational reference, perhaps such an attitude might be defensible as encouraging student responsibility, leadership, and expression. But educational values, communication with students, institutional concerns, and sound leadership training require a more positive role on the part of the faculty adviser. Swimming coaches do not teach swimming merely by throwing the novice into deep water. Much of the superficiality, lack of integrity, chicanery, authoritarianism, and cliquishness which have characterized some campus activities has developed because of the failure of the college, working through the faculty adviser, to give positive leadership to them.

Bloland has classified the adviser's functions into three areas: maintenance or custodial, group growth, and program content.[7] Under maintenance functions are those which help perpetuate the organization, follow rules and procedures, and provide a link with the group's history and traditions. The group growth functions refer to the adviser's contributions which help improve the operation and effectiveness of the group. These are essentially facilitating. They include: directing consideration toward and assisting with development of group participation skills; organizational structure and procedures; leadership training; effective planning; evaluation; and related topics which apply to groups regardless of their specific objectives.

It is in the third area, program content, that the faculty adviser makes his unique contribution as an educator in an institutional setting. Failure to help the group do more than maintain itself or carry on activities which are not related to the campus context is a deficiency on the part of the institution. Specific contributions which the faculty adviser can make in this area are offering program suggestions, recruiting colleagues to provide information and perspectives on issues, helping the members apply their classroom learning to out-of-class situations, and, in general, influencing the program and activities of the group so that they are compatible with objectives and endeavors of the college.

The effectiveness of a faculty adviser is determined more by the college community concept of his role than by any formal statement of duties or obligations. It is possible for a faculty adviser to operate democratically and still fulfill his educational responsibilities. The argument that a faculty adviser is dictatorial, authoritarian, and obstructive to the development of initiative and responsibility of students refers to his work methods, not to the position itself. Such characterizations can also be made of some classroom teachers, group leaders, politicians, and consultants in all kinds of enterprises. Not only must the faculty adviser have a clear perception

---

[7] Paul A. Bloland, "The Role of the Student Organization Adviser," *The Personnel and Guidance Journal,* XLI, No. 1 (September, 1962), 46.

of his role as an educational influence, but he and the entire institution must have a clearly defined philosophy regarding the role of activities. The two must go together for the most effective work with and through student groups. Without the support of the influential elements on any campus, the roles of activities and of faculty members who work with them are relegated, to use Woodrow Wilson's characterization, to the superficial, traditional position of side streets leading from the main street of education.

Practices on most campuses usually require a faculty member's agreement to serve in the role of adviser as a condition for recognition as an official college organization. One would normally expect a faculty adviser to share the opinions of, or, at least, to be in general agreement with the substantive beliefs and ideals of the campus organization he is to advise. This traditional expectancy has often made it difficult for some groups to find faculty advisers, because no members were willing to serve if such service implied total agreement with the group's purposes. Such cases arise most often with so-called controversial organizations advocating unpopular causes, or with social fraternities and sororities.

Activist groups particularly are finding it difficult to secure advisers where the climate of public opinion is especially antagonistic to the group and its teachings. Examples of such organizations are socialist and communist groups, pacifist organizations, campus affiliates of the various student civil rights organizations, etc. The Committee on Faculty Responsibility for the Academic Freedom of Students, of the American Association of University Professors, as well as the Academic Freedom Committee of the American Civil Liberties Union, opposed the denial of recognition to an organization on the basis of inability to find a faculty adviser. In view of the significant educational and liaison functions performed by such persons, however, colleges need to find a solution better than one that further weakens the educational relationship and communication between such groups and the host institutions.

One approach has been to re-define the role of the faculty adviser, to make it clear that acceptance of the advisership does not constitute endorsement of the group's views. Even in non-controversial situations, this clarification is important in order to achieve the most effective relationship between the faculty adviser and the student group he serves. The faculty council of Indiana University attempted to clarify this situation by changing the name of the position from "faculty adviser" to "faculty consultant," and by stating that his service as consultant is a form of assistance to students and does not imply approval of the purposes or activities of the organization.

An increasingly large number of organizations on campus have both faculty and students as members because many of the topics of concern to the current college generation are of mutual interest to scholars of all ages. This trend may eliminate the need for a faculty adviser, except as a representative for procedural matters. Civil rights groups, peace organizations, religious groups, political clubs, and recognition societies are typical campus groups falling into this category. They pose problems because often the members do not feel they should be governed by the rules and procedures pertaining to regular student organizations. The faculty members often unwittingly violate policies with regard to use of facilities, expenditures of funds, or use of the college's name in activities. However, from the educational point of view, this intermingling of faculty and student members is highly desirable. The administrative response will need to be greater flexibility, careful interpretation of the reasons for rules and procedures, and encouragement to the faculty members to stimulate student members to greater intellectual involvement and responsible scholarship.

Procedures Regarding Student Organizations and Activities

Until very recently the process by which a new student organization was established seemed clear and simple. A group of students would talk with the dean, elect some temporary officers, write up a constitution, organize permanently, file the information in the dean's office, and be in business. What constituted a student group seemed clear, and the procedures seemed appropriate. But the rise of organizations engaged in political and social action off-campus, and increased interest in national and international affairs have made traditional procedures and terminology inadequate. Many of the difficulties experienced on campuses spring from the very desirable trend to relate the college to the world around it and to eliminate every vestige of a cloister. Desirable or not, however, the student personnel administrator and his college have had to face a variety of problems. Defining groups, clarifying obligations of groups which have affiliations with national bodies, maintaining privacy while still discharging managerial and educational obligations, determining policies about speakers, and regulating assemblies and demonstrations have necessitated responses to new conditions with philosophically sound policies and procedures capable of withstanding intense and often antagonistic analysis.

Meaning of collegiate affiliation. In question is the very designation used in describing those organizations which have met college requirements. The traditional "approved" or "recognized" imply a degree of sponsorship often not intended. For example, some institutions feel it is improper to call a Marxist organization "approved." Yet under their regulations, groups of students studying or advocating extremist views have a right to organize and to use college facilities; thus some term is necessary. "Recognized" avoids some of the connotation implied in the word "approved." Some institutions have begun to use the term "registered," which implies still less sponsorship. Regardless of the specific term used, it is important to have a clear statement regarding the meaning of college recognition, what rights and privileges such organizations have, and the responsibilities the organization and its members assume when they apply for and receive the college's designation. Students as individual citizens may join organizations which are not affiliated with the college, such as the Elks, Masons, the city branch of the NAACP, or the local Reserve Officers Association and, as such, are not under college rules and regulations except those pertaining to all students. But the members of the college chapter of a fraternity, college branch of the NAACP, or the college unit of the ROTC, are consequently answerable to rules and policies pertaining to official organizations of the sponsoring institution.

The American Association of University Professors, the American Civil Liberties Union, and many other educational organizations feel that students should be free to organize and join any legal groups of their choosing. The essential nature and the activities of a college environment should encourage a serious examination of ideas, a vigorous discussion of current issues, and an uninhibited hypothesizing or "thinking out loud." Therefore, the college's attitude must be as broad, flexible and open-minded as possible. There is a distinction, however, to be made between the right of an individual student to join community groups, and the need for the organization of those groups on the campus.

Social action organizations and activities. College activities are simultaneously the result, as well as the creators, of social forces. As the result, they mirror the expectations and perceptions of college life perpetuated by traditional student organizations and by the images conveyed to young and old alike through popular media, folklore, alumni tales, and campus and social value systems. As creators of social forces, however, they can influence to a great extent the activities which are acceptable, the ideas which are under consideration, and the methods of expression which are found on a given campus. An institution can merely reflect the society from which the students come or which has created it. Or it can be a truly educational force which stimulates and facilitates introspection concerning ideas and values, and thus becomes a part of the development of its students and the society of which they are a part. If activities are to be assigned an educational role, it is an obligation of the student personnel worker to encourage them as creators of social forces, rather than mere reflections of the bland values and traditions of either the current student body or contempory society.

Faculty involvement in making policies for student activities. Faculty members should participate in the establishment of policies pertaining to student activities, since these are an integral part of the college educational program. Some student personnel workers have, consciously or unconsciously, assumed complete responsibility for the establishment and enforcement of such policies. The result, in many institutions, has been a cleavage between the administrators and faculty about specific policies. Students quickly sense differences or feelings in such instances and play one segment of the college community against another.

Questions concerning such topics as appropriate classroom dress, campus behavior, free speech, free assembly, picketing, demonstrations, and guest speakers require a total institutional approach. The most effective practice seems to call for a student affairs committee composed of students, faculty members, and administrators which forms policies, evaluates programs, and stimulates activities and groups contributing to the achievement of educational objectives. The policies made by this group are usually subject to review by the college's board of trustees. Most boards need and appreciate the leadership and groundwork of a body speaking for the campus. In many situations, student personnel administrators must take the initiative to have such representative bodies organized.

Tradition, custom, and strong personalities have often permitted or forced monolithic administrative structures, which seem to work well until fundamental issues arise. Then the absence of faculty-student involvement and an educationally unsound situation become all too evident. The freedom from joint policy-making groups, which some students seem to want and some faculty members and administrators seem willing to support, is illusory and a disintegrative influence on the campus. Involvement of all segments of the community through discussion, debate, resolution of differences, recognition of responsibility by participation, and the existence of recognized procedures strengthen a high quality educational program within an institution.

Maintaining membership rosters. Traditionally, many colleges have attempted to maintain records of the members of its various student groups. These lists were usually submitted by the officers and filed by the college without verification. Often, only the lists of original or founding members were filed. In many cases the period of membership was not specified nor the degree of involvement indicated. During and following World War II, the trend toward investigating past actions and beliefs of individuals raised numerous questions regarding the validity and propriety of maintaining such records. They served no useful educational purpose, in most cases, and became increasingly difficult to maintain as activities multiplied and the number of participants grew. A change has come about as a result of many causes: the burdensome clerical loads, the failure to use the records in any meaningful educational way, and questions regarding the propriety and validity of reporting memberships and presumed beliefs and activities years later. In general practice the sole requirement is that names of current officers only be filed for communication purposes. In those instances where lists are maintained for counseling and eligibility purposes, the practice has grown of discarding them annually or when the new officers or members are reported.

Student Government

Probably the greatest handicap to securing educational benefits from student government is the term itself. In practically all American colleges and universities student government is in reality "participation in institutional government." The difference lies in the perception of the role, not in semantics. If one perceives the role of student government as the exercise of complete and final regulation of a specified area of collegiate life, the question immediately becomes "What is our authority and over what areas are we autonomous?" Unfortunately for the typically competent, eager, and aggressive student leader, the answer to the questions is most disappointing. In most situations, the only authority and autonomy student government agencies have are those delegated to them by the governing board of the institution.

If, however, one perceives the role of student government as participation in the government of the institution, its authority and autonomy are usually limited only by the competence and energy of the students themselves. From the student personnel point of view, it is important to interpret constantly the difference between legal authority and *de facto* authority.

Once the role and perception of student government is clarified, the operational challenge to the adviser becomes one of stimulating, encouraging, and even pushing officers and participants to exercise the authority they have, because recognition and status arise from effective work and not from verbalized statements.

A second important aspect of clarifying the perception of student government is defining its scope to include residence units and specialized bodies in addition to the central, all-campus senate and office of student body president. The student government functions of resident unit officers, Interfraternity Council, Panhellenic Association, Union Board of Directors, Association of Women Students, Student Court, and similar bodies are of the utmost significance in achieving the objectives of student government; yet, all too often, they are overlooked as student government agencies by students and staff alike.

A third significant aspect of student government which needs constant attention is realizing that the most important single factor in its success, whether it be in residence halls, fraternities and sororities, or on the all-campus level, is the quality of leadership given to it by students and the institution, not its formal structure. On all too many campuses, student government workers spend their time constantly amending the constitution in a vain hope of finding the organizational structure which will assure its automatic success. With effective leadership by students and faculty, almost any system of student government will make significant contributions to the institution; without effective leadership, including support and recognition by the college, every system will be just another activity.

The objectives of student government include: facilitating communication among various segments of the campus; increasing the student's identification with the college and his feeling of personal responsibility for learning and development by involving him in making decisions about his collegiate life and behavior; providing experience and participation in self government as a part of citizenship and leadership development; and providing a method for meaningfully relating various student activities to each other. The wording or classification of these objectives is not as important as the points they emphasize—communication, involvement, educationally sound experience, and order, instead of self-defeating competition, duplication, or even chaos. The challenge to the student personnel worker is to interpret these objectives to other administrators, faculty members and students so that their perception of student government broadens to appreciate its full educational significance. Such a foundation then becomes the basis for sound leadership training, cooperation, integration of effort, and positive relationships among all aspects of the college.

Group Work on the College Campus

The space limitations of an introductory, descriptive statement do not permit a full discussion of the techniques and methodology of group work, to use a social service term. Furthermore, some educators and writers may feel a repugnance at emphasizing methods of working with individuals through groups. The personnel worker, of all people in society, must lead the fight against conformity, group stultification, and the mediocre standard. A clever phrase, perceptive polemic, or a breast-thumping cry against the pressures of modern civilization will not solve the problems of anonymity, socialization, personal growth through experience, and alienation from any values which the personnel worker must face in his professional work daily on most college campuses. Thus, to remain ignorant of principles which underlie effective education, in the belief that doing nothing is better, is a serious abdication of responsibility.

Generally speaking, group work can be seen from at least three aspects: (1) as an educational force integrating the student's out-of-class activities and energy with the institution's academic program; (2) as a technique or method in student activities to broaden their outreach, increase their effectiveness, and assist in developing leadership and participation skills; and (3) as a management aid in working with large groups of individuals.

Practically all colleges, even the smallest, classify or group students, whether or not they consciously use effective group work procedures. Thus, any debate over the use of modern group techniques is an academic one, since the reality of the situation makes it imperative for the student personnel worker to recognize the situation calling for group techniques and to know how to use them.

The effective use of campus groups multiplies the efforts and focuses the impact of the institution by providing a bridge whereby it can come into contact with the individual student. The leaders of the various groups become communication links with their members and, through them, with large numbers of other students. Failure on the part of the college to establish a positive relationship with campus groups magnifies the anonymity of individual students and the impersonality of the relationship between students and the institution. Thus, student personnel workers on every campus have, as a major responsibility, the task of improving the functioning of groups as groups, and of applying to the campus situation the wide range of group techniques—goal clarification, effective induction of new members, role identification, continuous evaluation, training, and assisting groups and their advisers to establish productive relationships.

Summary

This chapter has emphasized that the primary factor in maximizing the educational value of group activities is perception of its role by the college. If seen as an omni-present evil to be controlled but otherwise ignored, little educational value will be realized. If perceived as a significant educational force, much too valuable to be neglected, they can become an important and integral aspect of the institution's total program. Second in importance only to the clarification of the role of activities is the perception of and importance attached to the position of faculty adviser to campus organizations and activities. The function of the adviser is to serve as the liaison or link between the formal educational program of the institution and the informal, out-of-class program represented by campus groups and activities. Details of specific procedures, regulations, and programs may vary greatly and still contribute significantly to the achievement of important educational objectives, after the foundation has been laid by establishing a sound institutional philosophy and defining the faculty relationship to campus activities. The essential job of the student personnel worker in this area, therefore, is to lead his college in these two important steps, and contribute his technical skills and professional knowledge to the fulfillment of these tasks.

CHAPTER VIII

Current Issues and Trends in Student Personnel Work

The changing nature of today's colleges and universities has made it imperative for administrators to examine existing educational programs with a view toward meeting the needs of society and, more particularly, the needs of the students they serve. The adaptations and innovations of recent years, responding to such forces as the greater number of students and demands for specialized programs, have created problems and raised issues concerning educational policy and practice. Student personnel programs, as part of the total educational enterprise, have not escaped the pitfalls of crisis management. To be able to formulate a positive program for the future, the personnel dean must be alert to current issues and emerging trends.

Students as the Focus of Education

Student unrest leaped to the attention of the American public during the school year 1964–65 with a shocking force. From the East to the West Coast campus events at the nation's very best colleges and universities forced educators particularly, and the public in general, to realize that all was not well on the educational scene. Regardless of specific details, it became evident to even the casual observer that feelings of anonymity, frustration, mistrust, and alienation from the commonly verbalized goals of the educational community characterized a significant segment of the student body. Further analysis revealed that these feelings were not just a passing fad nor the result of skilled agitators, but were fed by the nature of the educational process on all too many college campuses throughout the country.

President Logan Wilson of the American Council on Education warned that the student was in danger of becoming the forgotten man of higher education, that he was being engulfed and ignored by the "knowledge industry" that American colleges and universities were becoming.[1] He further warned that, if the de-personalization of the student was allowed to go unchecked and unchallenged, it would present a grave threat to the very purposes of higher education. He decried the fact that faculty and administration (committed to teaching) had placed a low value on their students' abilities and potentialities as scholars, a fact which does not escape the attention of students, and further contributes to low morale, resentment, and antagonism.

The student personnel worker is engulfed daily with problems coming out of such forces as the increased enrollment, faculty abdication of responsibility for student life and extra-class learning, complex and contradictory demands and pressures from parents, alumni, public, and students, and the increasing heterogeneity of the college population. He frequently responds by becoming a technician wrestling with day-to-day problems and emergencies rather than serving his true role of being a staff member in the educational process. In the years immediately ahead, if higher education is to be enabled to remove the student and his learning from the periphery of significant college activity and restore them as the first order of business, the student personnel function must serve in a role much greater than that of providing technical and professional services. The first step in assuming this role is to have student personnel become an integral part of the institution.

Integration of the Student Personnel Program With the Total Life of the Institution

The various services the student personnel program offers exists not merely to control students so that they can be educated in the classroom; rather, they exist to provide an environment which stimulates and motivates them in the direction of the institutional objective. This brings student personnel a major problem—that of integrating its work with the total life of the institution, thereby unifying rather than segmenting academic life and extra-class life. As emphasized throughout the preceding chapters, it is particularly

[1] *Higher Education and National Affairs,* XIII, 32 (Washington, D.C.: American Council on Education, October 23, 1964), 7.

important that student personnel functions be seen in their positive, educational role, and not be perceived as externally imposed services having little relationship to the primary function of the college.

Unfortunately, the organizational structure in many colleges has led to an artificial separation of duties for administrative purposes. The structure has frequently led to a classification of problems into academic, public relations, student personnel, or business areas. Such a separation handicaps the coordinated use of resources on the campus. These resources are needed to meet the many problems faced by students as individuals and by the institution as an entity; moreover, a situation has resulted in which many faculty members and administrators disclaim responsibility for the student's total life and, by such abdication, force sole concern for out-of-class life, extra-curricular learning, and student behavior upon personnel deans.

Even more harmful to the effective operation of the student personnel program has been the widespread perception of the program as a control or a disciplinary device rather than as an educational force. Such a view not only handicaps student personnel workers in performing their educational functions but limits whatever contribution they might make on campus.

Administrative structure and size of an institution are not alone the factors causing the loss of "individualizing" higher education. While these may have some impact, two other factors center about the institution's commitment to the student: To what extent does the institution assist an individual student in developing a concept of himself as a motivated, self-directing person? To what degree does the university stimulate him to use the resources of the college community to achieve his objectives—which hopefully are at least compatible, if not identical, with those of the institution?

Faculty, students, and administration all must be involved in policy-making and programming if student personnel's aim of integrating the total life of the institution is to be reached. Merely verbalizing about the importance of extra-curricular life does not necessarily insure its full understanding by faculty and students. Rather, faculty members must actively take part in evaluating, supervising, and directing this aspect of college life as they would in formulating their own curricular program. Otherwise, extra-curricular life will not become an integral part of the educational process.

This area cannot be left to personnel workers as if it were their responsibility alone.

Students also must be led to understand how legitimate and necessary the faculty and administration responsibility is in maintaining the quality of extra-curricular life. Students should participate in developing a quality program which is complementary to the standards of the institution and not carve out allegedly private areas which they assert are not legitimate concerns of the institution.

Thus one of the most significant upcoming challenges that educational administration, in general, and student personnel, in particular, will have to meet is that of reversing the trend toward fragmentation on the campus. Procedures and programs will have to be devised which will encourage the involvement and effective interaction of all segments of the campus community in determining the institutional impact upon the student.

Institutional Nature and Characteristics

Basic to centering institutional life around the student is a careful examination and reaffirmation of the essential characteristics of the college itself. Due to fast-moving events on the higher educational scene, many institutions have, in fact, become something different from what they thought they were or from what they claim to be in their catalogs. Students who enter a college under a misapprehension regarding its nature have a basis for protest. If a college, however, has clearly defined its goals, values, and essential characteristics, and has interpreted them carefully to new students and faculty members alike, there is little basis for resentment, rebellion, or rejection of its standards and ideals. Everyone involved must understand that the goals of an institution are their goals. When they do, immature rebellion by students and low morale and unrest among faculty members will be reduced to a minimum. Much of the current unrest among students and faculty alike stems from a failure on the part of colleges to determine and interpret their dominant characteristics in a positive and effective manner. As a result, rapid student and faculty turnover results in misconceptions regarding the role and objectives of the college.

Self-Study and Evaluation

In response to the changes in student bodies and the demands of society, many institutions are undergoing self-evaluation, effecting administrative and curricular reorganization, and making other adjustments in an effort to meet modern requirements. It is essential that those staff members related to student personnel be involved in this process, even if they have to make their contributions independent of the formal evaluation committee. All too often, personnel deans in particular have been perceived by the faculty, alumni, and others as defenders of the *status quo,* resisting changes in rules, procedures, and regulations until the absurdity of this position comes to a point where modifications or clarifications of policy must be made. Personnel deans are often omitted from membership on study committees. However, because of their daily association and intimate familiarity with student needs, problems, and characteristics, the student personnel staff must lead the way when studying the impact various changing conditions have made on higher education and how changing student characteristics affect the college community.

A self-study process should review and clarify the proper roles and relationships, one to the other, of students, faculty, administrators, trustees, and alumni, in establishing and administering policies and procedures for extra-class life. Particular attention should be given to methods of downgrading the influence of negative and contradictory aspects of the community. There is a continual demand from classroom teachers for the personnel worker to cut down on parties, eliminate automobiles, reduce the role of social organizations, and relegate athletics to a proper status within the institution. Such steps fall flat if based upon the assumption that students will automatically study harder. Efforts to redirect social forces on a campus must be taken jointly by all segments of the campus community with reasonable agreement upon the goal being sought. Then with a clear goal as a guideline jointly arrived at and supported, whatever steps are taken will not be perceived as imposed by external authoritarians—the all-too-often misconception of student personnel.

Institutional Flexibility and Attention to Individual Student Needs

The most important emphasis in curricular or administrative reorganization is in providing for institutional flexibility and for meeting the needs of individual students. Yet, all too often, such programs lead to the rigorous and unthinking application of requirements originally established in the interest of balance, depth, and scholarship. Irritating, energy-wasting conferences often bring about relaxation of specific regulations, but only after harmful discussions and clashes which negate the very impact which the standards and rules originally attempted to convey.

With regard to student life in particular, rules and procedures should be carefully evaluated from the standpoint of increasing student responsibility and toward decreasing faculty and staff involvement in detailed matters that interfere with their important counseling and teaching duties. While academic requirements and procedures should not be used to eliminate the need for faculty members and administrators to make decisions, neither should they be eliminated because of fear about what decisions these staff members will make if they had the freedom and responsibility to make them. Better prepared students, committed teachers, and skilled faculty advisers require rules which are primarily guidelines and not definite, rigid standards.

Communication on the Campus

The fact that many problems on the modern college campus are caused by faulty communication has been acknowledged frequently in recent years. Almost any analysis of campus problems reveals that misunderstanding, confusion, or conflicts of goals resulted from communication failures. Rapid turnover among faculty members has exaggerated the problem, considerably; because, frequently, when a new student is taught by a new faculty member, both are puzzled by contradictions in the college situation and both are unaware of the reasons for many traditional student activities and customs. Even in the small college there are striking differences in the perception by students and faculty alike of various aspects of college life.

Communication with faculty. The need for effective orientation of new *students* has been emphasized in Chapter Two. The effective orientation of new *faculty* members is often neglected on many campuses. On the small college campus it is assumed that new faculty members will automatically understand and adopt the goals, standards, and ideals of their new institution. On the large college campus, the failure to orient new members is often due to an oversight, or the pressure of other tasks and problems. Even on those campuses where the induction of the new faculty member is a conscious project, the program often makes him feel like a neophyte and a recruit, and it often fails to assist him in seeing what is expected of him.

The student personnel worker must understand that it is necessary for him to constantly interpret his work to other university personnel. Wherever this interpretation is not continuously carried forward, many staff members sincerely wonder what the student personnel worker thinks he is accomplishing by certain rules and regulations. Even on the small college campus it is important to have periodic meetings in which other staff members may secure information, clarify questions, or provide information which the student personnel worker urgently needs in his work. Failure to establish formal and informal channels of communication often results in situations which make it appear that the student personnel worker is, in effect, an empire builder. In turn, the personnel worker often develops the idea that only he is concerned about student values.

Communication among student personnel specialists. Another important aspect of the communication process on most campuses is communication among the various specialists who are performing student personnel functions. Often the doctor in the health service, the financial aids officer, the counselor, the personnel dean, and the residence hall supervisor, all come into contact with some phase of a student's problems but fail to communicate among themselves. Such failure creates feelings of suspicion, lack of confidence, and even antagonism. It should be axiomatic that when two or more people are involved in work which relates to a specific individual, they should have formal and informal means of communicating among themselves. While most people feel they have sufficient informal means of communication, they realize, too, that the increase of routine work, the growth in size of student bodies, changes in staff, and a constant turnover of students, all diminish the effectiveness of informal communication and all these factors underscore the need for the establishment of official channels, such as a personnel council and periodic staff meetings.

On most campuses all staff members having responsibility for some aspect of student work need regularly scheduled staff meetings, carefully written job descriptions, formalized statements of goals and purposes for the various functions, and periodic reports among themselves, in order to keep effectively informed. Without these formal procedures, some staff members simply do not know or understand what other colleagues are attempting to do with the result that there is suspicion, duplication, or friction. Asking a staff member to write out his perceptions of the goals and functions of some other office or staff member is an administrative technique which reveals how great the need for such communication is.

Communication among students. Effective communication at the student level presents a great challenge to student personnel workers. Communication is important not only between students and the administration and between students and the faculty, but just as significantly to that among students themselves. Research on campus cultures has revealed the significant influence one student has upon another. It has also revealed the existence of sub-cultures which interpret the campus scene in different ways to the various sub-groups on a campus. Thus, the duty of communication is to explain and interpret campus life in order to support the objectives of the institution and thus to counteract the influence of explanations and interpretations which handicap their achievement. Communications among undergraduates is never lacking when a beauty queen is announced, or an athlete makes the grade, or a campus politician impresses his colleagues. But, all too often, communication is lacking when it comes to telling how great the rewards from scholastic achievement can be, or what the nature of true scholarship is, or how desirable it is to acquire breadth in learning. Thus, any attempt to improve communication, whether it be through more effective orientation for new students or through continuous communication of the ideals and values of the institution, must come out of those same channels through which undergraduates are accustomed to receiving the messages which count.

Student leaders are among the most significant communication links. Others come about from the classroom professor's side comments and topics of conversation; the items featured in student newspapers and on the local radio programs; the work of faculty advisers with student committees; the stance of the governing board and top administrators regarding discussion of current issues; and the views of alumni.

A constant problem concerning communication channels is in evaluating the validity of comments and reports received through them. As one administrator phrased it, "How can you tell there is a need for improved communication before a problem becomes critical and needless harm has been done?" Clearly, every report of ineffective teaching is not valid, but whenever it is authentic, there must be that first report or feedback regarding it. Much of the challenge in this area to the educational administrator is the interpretation of the seemingly contradictory and petty reports, and the application of them to the broad scope of the institution.

Issues of Student Freedom and Responsibility

One of the areas which exemplifies the communication problem at its most difficult level is that of student freedoms. Most colleges, on the one hand, feel that they stand for certain ideals and values which their students should reflect in their daily lives, and that, in recognition of the influence of the total environment, they should regulate at least its dominant aspects. Moreover, colleges feel that their environment reflects, as well as affects, the total institution. Therefore, they conclude, students' likes notwithstanding, that the college must assume and exercise responsibility for that environment, including students' behavior, even in non-academic activities. Many students, on the other hand, sincerely cannot understand why any institution feels it has a right to regulate their private lives. "It is simply a question of rights," asserted the editor of *The Michigan Daily*. "What right does the university have to interfere with the personal life of a student?"[2] He further claimed that rules imposed on students without their consent are unjustified. Frequently, the student personnel worker receives the impression that students want freedom from practically all restraints and obligations before they will undertake any mature and responsible behavior. Students today

[2] *The Detroit Free Press,* February 4, 1962, sec. C, p. 1.

have more freedom in their personal, social, and intellectual endeavors than at any time in history. Yet many believe that they need even more freedom before they can express themselves sufficiently, or can demonstrate initiative, develop creativity, and truly manifest maturity and responsibility.

What is the true situation? President Hugh Borton of Haverford College described the situation by saying:

> [Students] insist on greater freedom from interference by the administration in all aspects of college life and at the same time insist that there be developed closer contacts between the students on the one hand and faculty and administration on the other. . . . They wish for greater individual instruction and advocate higher faculty salaries and more faculty appointments without realizing that to do all these things requires vastly increased financial resources, including higher tuition charges to which they object.[3]
>
> . . . But we would be making the worst possible mistake for the future of academic freedom on our campuses if we were to blind ourselves to the legitimate appeals of students for improved conditions in undergraduate education simply because we see inconsistencies in their positions.[4]

He also stated that it was especially important that college administrators and faculty members not wait for students' protests before doing anything about the problems.

The United States National Student Association has led much of the attack upon the concept of *in loco parentis*. A basic policy decision of the association declares:

> *USNSA* condemns the tradition of *in loco parentis* and the educational habits and practices it justifies . . . (it) permits arbitrary and extensive repression of student pursuits and thereby impairs the total significance of the university as a center for the conflict of ideas.
>
> . . . Paternalism in any form induces or reinforces immaturity, conformity, and disinterest among those whose imagination, critical talent, and capacities for integrity and growth should be encouraged and given opportunity for development.
>
> Insofar as *in loco parentis* doctrine removes responsibility for personal decision-making from the individual student, it distorts and weakens a significant phase of the educational process. The

---

[3] In an address to the National Association of Student Personnel Administrators, April 5, 1965, quoted in the *Proceedings of the Forty-Seventh Anniversary Conference*, p. 79.

[4] *Ibid.*, p. 80.

unexamined acceptance of authority which is often appropriate to the child-parent relationship must be replaced in the universities by the encouragement of a critical and dialectical relationship between the student and his community. The range of inquiry within or beyond the classroom must not be restricted out of paternal considerations but must be opened out of educational ones.[5]

Neal Johnston, then Director of the Academic Freedom Project of the Association added the intellectual aspect by stating,

> . . . the trauma of suddenly finding oneself independent is no greater than the trauma of suddenly finding Marx, or any other articulate social critic. It is no more dangerous to wander the streets alone at night than it is to wander alone through the library stacks. Education is an adult business, and those who are going through the process, should be regarded and treated as adults.[6]

A further aspect of the student freedom issue is that of political expression and involvement in political and social action. The AAUP Committee S report states that:

> Students and student organizations should be free to discuss all questions of interest to them and to express opinions publicly or privately without penalty, to promote the causes they support by distributing literature, circulating petitions, picketing or taking any other peaceful action on or off the campus . . . Students should be free to organize and join associations for educational, political, religious, or cultural purposes. The fact of affiliation with any extramural association or national organization or political party, if it is an open affiliation, should not, of itself, bar a group from recognition.[7]

The response of the student personnel worker to these issues must be carefully weighed if he is not to be in the position of William Berkeley, Governor of Virginia in the 17th century, who was quoted, "Thank God there are no free schools or printing . . . for learning has brought disobedience and heresy . . . into the world, and printing has divulged them . . . God keep us from both."[8]

The student personnel worker must strive to introduce objectiv-

---

[5] *Codification of Policy 1961–1962* (Philadelphia, Pa.: U.S. National Student Association, 1962), p. 31.

[6] *Seminar Working Papers for the Fifteenth National Student Congress* (Philadelphia, Pa.: U.S. National Student Association, 1962), p. 52.

[7] "Report of Committee S on Faculty Responsibility for the Academic Freedom of Students," *AAUP Bulletin*, 50, No. 3 (1964), 255. *See also Bulletin* 51, No. 5 (1965), 447–449.

[8] Quoted in Carl L. Becker, *Freedom and Responsibility in the American Way of Life* (New York: Vintage Books, Alfred A. Knopf, Inc., 1955), p. 51.

ity and intellectual honesty into discussions about this issue in which he is normally ego-involved. If he can exemplify the qualities for which a college should stand, neither student morals nor institutional standards will suffer. Rather, a democratic philosophy and sound educational practice will be strengthened by allowing vigorous debate with representatives of this generation of college students who are impatient, idealistic, extremely verbal, and highly competent. Blind adherence to the *status quo* or dogged reaffirmation of rules and policies will not add to the educational contributions of the issue.

Issues Pertaining to the Organization and Administration of Student Personnel Services

Student personnel services do not comprise a single unified operation. They are, instead, a number of relatively independent functions, all contributing toward the achievement of the common goal of making the student and his needs the focal point of educational effort. The question of the proper organization and administration of these services, therefore, involves finding the most effective method of establishing and providing them on a campus. There is no *one* plan of organizational structure which will meet the diverse needs or which will serve the interests of all institutions and their students.

An important challenge student personnel administrators must meet is organizing and administering their services in such a way that the staff members who are concerned with the various activities feel constantly stimulated to intellectual and professional growth, and thereby find their work a meaningful contribution—in the light of the value and reward system—to the particular college community. As previously noted, student personnel staff members are, in reality, faculty and staff members of the college. Their loyalty usually is to their own department and they receive direction for their personnel work from other sources. This means that administrative structure must coordinate and integrate the efforts of those people who are essentially volunteer workers.

Centralization versus de-centralization. It is not necessarily the size of the institution that presents the issues concerning the degree of centralization needed in student personnel administration.

On many small campuses the student personnel worker in the central office is bogged down with appointments, conferences regarding rule violations, and other office work, to the detriment of his larger functions. Similarly, on the large campus, the central student personnel administrator, who has not delegated sufficiently, is bogged down with endless interviews, administrative tasks, and paper work. The real issues to be resolved are giving effective direction to the program and implementing a basic philosophy to guide the administration of student services. On the larger campus the issue is one of delegating sufficient function and responsibility to residence or activities centers, where the staff members are in first-hand contact with students and their leaders. On the small campus, the issue is one of formulating an effective administrative policy without limiting the freedom, flexibility, and initiative of those staff members who work on a day-to-day basis with students and other staff members.

In most cases, the issue is that of determining whether the desirability for centralizing the administrative concern for student personnel services should be under one person, such as a dean of students, or under two coordinate heads, such as a dean of men and a dean of women. While this is an over-simplification of all the administrative issues concerned with the problem, the answer seems to depend upon the objectives set by the administrative structure on a particular campus. If the objective is to relieve the president from detailed involvement in a large number of student personnel matters, it would seem desirable to have one major administrator appointed to head up the entire field and report to the president. If, on the other hand, the objective on a particular campus is to secure broader administrative supervision, to involve top level staff members, maintain certain public relationship objectives, there appears to be no advantage in establishing a single administrator. In centralization, careful attention must be given to those student personnel services which are not traditionally classified as falling under one sex or the other. Top student personnel administrators often are separated to serve a certain sex. This is traditional. Yet under such a condition, other matters such as training faculty advisers, developing counseling services, stimulating and supervising all-campus student government, initiating residence programs for both sexes, encouraging greater intellectual depth in extra-curricular activities, and striving to involve more faculty members in this extra-curricular life, may not receive proper attention or the priority needed for their development.

Providing effective personnel services for students with special needs. As student bodies become more heterogeneous and campuses grow larger in physical size and broader in academic programs, the student personnel administrator is faced with the increasingly difficult problem of meeting the needs of specialized segments of students: the foreign, the graduate, the married, the potentially superior, the culturally disadvantaged, the commuting, and the physically handicapped. Effective administration requires a certain degree of conformity, standardization, and parallel structure. Yet the special needs of certain groups of students require services which cut across the usual organizational lines or which require much greater individual attention than a particular office is equipped to provide. The answer to this problem, in addition to careful administrative coordination, lies in the efficient mobilization of all community resources to help meet the needs of this special group. Faculty wives, church groups, service clubs, faculty members with special interests, and alumni, all potentially are rich resources which, if tapped, could assist the college in enriching its student personnel program and could help meet the needs of the specialized segments of the student body without lowering the quality of services in general.

Meeting demands for expanded services. The administrator is continually torn by two competing forces. On the one hand, by the tremendous pressure for him to place the student more on his own and to decrease traditional services. On the other hand, by the increasing need for him to offer more and more counseling services to the student. The administrator is hard pressed to interpret to his academic and faculty colleagues his needs within the student personnel program without appearing to be an empire builder or seemingly to be wasteful of scarce institutional funds. Certainly, expanding student bodies demand greater services. The trend, however, seems to be very clear. Student services cannot be expected to expand in proportion to quantitative growth. The administrator must evaluate very critically the services expected from his staff and organize his resources to provide those expected by the institution. Further, he must see the importance of marshalling the resources of the total community to help meet the needs of the campus, rather than striving to build a staff which alone attempts to meet all these demands.

Evaluating student personnel programs and services. The process of evaluating the effectiveness and quality of any program or service is a continual one. Informal evaluation should be a day-to-day process. Most campus situations, however, require periodic formal evaluation, necessary if the programs are to be kept alert and flexible. Evaluating personnel services is an extremely difficult process because the results are non-quantitative. Creativity and ingenuity are essential prerequisites for developing methods which will measure and offer ways to improve the effectiveness of the services.[9]

Maintaining a balanced student personnel program. In the age of specialization, fads, public relations appeals, and rapidly changing needs, it is difficult for the student personnel administrator to maintain a balanced student personnel program and, at the same time, resist forces which demand services disproportionate to campus needs. From an administrative point of view, all student services should be developed and staffed on the basis of an over-all plan, consciously designed to meet the needs and objectives of the institution. All too frequently, however, certain services are brought into the limelight because of some emergency, the possibility of securing special funds, publicity over a particular problem, or the appeal of a particularly competent, persuasive staff member. Long range plans based on projected enrollments and needs should be flexible enough to serve as guidelines yet firm enough to resist the temporary pressures and demands of passing problems.

There are many other problems facing the student personnel administrator as he attempts to devise a structure that will meet the needs of a particular college campus. Specialists in any particular discipline, whether it be within student personnel or in the broader academic field, tend to see problems from the point of view of their own field. The administrator must force himself to view problems and issues from the perspective of the total institution and its overall objectives. Within the student personnel field, he must increase

---

[9] *See* C. Gilbert Wrenn, *Student Personnel Work in College* (New York: Ronald Press, 1951), pp. 476–477; Robert B. Kamm, "An Inventory of Student Reaction to Student Personnel Services," *Educational and Psychological Measurement,* X, 3 (1950), 537–544; Eric N. Rackham, *Student Personnel Services Inventory* (Kent, Ohio: Kent State University, 1963).

the effectiveness of his administrative structure without making excessive demands upon the institution's resources.

Professional Associations in the Student Personnel Field

Professional associations in the student personnel field serve important functions in disseminating information, and contributing to the continued personal and professional growth of their members (through conferences, publications, and activities). These services are particularly important in helping the student personnel worker, whose daily work often affords little time for research, reading, or participation in activities beyond his own campus. Student activities and problems are remarkably similar from campus to campus. Therefore, the alert student personnel worker seizes upon every opportunity to keep himself informed and to establish personal relationships with his counterparts on other campuses.

There is a wide variety of organizations serving the general and specialized interests of student personnel workers.[10] Those of greatest general interest to the administrator are the American College Personnel Association, the National Association of Student Personnel Administrators, and the National Association of Women Deans and Counselors. Organizations appealing to workers in specialized areas include the Conference of Jesuit Student Personnel Administrators, the American Association of Collegiate Registrars and Admissions Officers, the Association of College Unions, and the National Association of Foreign Student Affairs. Since the demands of the rapidly changing field of student personnel require more than general knowledge and good intentions, educators, who have been assigned student personnel responsibilities, should not ignore this important source of aid but should affiliate with and participate in the activities of these professional associations.

---

[10] The fifth annual addition (September, 1965) of *The Directory of Student Personnel and Related Organizations in Colleges and Universities,* issued by the National Association of Student Personnel Administrators, lists 40 organizations and 24 journals and newsletters in the field of student personnel. This publication is available from the NASPA through its Secretary-Treasurer, Dean Carl W. Knox, Dean of Men, University of Illinois, Urbana, Illinois.

Summary

The field of student personnel work grew out of the needs of an increasingly heterogeneous student body in a vastly complex system of higher education in America. Therefore, it is of utmost importance that the student personnel worker keep abreast of current changes and respond to the overall situation with creativity and ingenuity. The years ahead will demand their evolving new approaches to problems and devising new methods to answer them. This will involve all segments of the campus community in order to achieve their goal of educating individuals to their greatest potential. Student personnel services have much to contribute to higher education, but they must be as alert, as scholarly, and as effective as the most outstanding academic department if they are to be a truly educational force.

Bibliography

Babbidge, Homer D., Jr., *Student Financial Aid.* Washington, D.C.: American College Personnel Association, 1960.

Bakken, Clarence J., *The Legal Basis for College Student Personnel Work.* Washington, D.C.: American College Personnel Association, 1961.

Brady, T. A., and L. F. Snoxell, *Student Discipline in Higher Education.* Washington, D.C.: American College Personnel Association, 1965.

Brammer, Lawrence M., and Everett L. Shostrom, *Therapeutic Psychology.* Englewood Cliffs, N.J.: Prentice Hall, Inc., 1960.

Bricks and Mortarboards, A Report on College Planning and Building. New York: Educational Facilities Laboratories, 1964.

Brown, Nicholas C., ed., *Orientation to College Learning—A Reappraisal.* Washington, D.C.: American Council on Education, 1961.

Brownell, Baker, "Higher Education and the Community: The Identification of Learning with Living." *Journal of Higher Education,* XXX, No. 9 (1959), 469–480.

Burns, Gerald P., ed., *Administrators in Higher Education: Their Functions and Coordination.* New York: Harper and Bros., 1962.

Carson, John J., *Governance of Colleges and Universities.* New York: McGraw-Hill Book Company, 1960.

Cowley, W. H., "The History of Student Residential Housing." *School and Society,* XL, No. 1040 (1934), 705–712.

Eddy, Edward D., *The College Influence on Student Character.* Washington, D.C.: American Council on Education, 1959.

Eells, Walter C., and Ernest V. Hollis, *Student Financial Aid in Higher Education: An Annotated Bibliography,* U.S. Department of Health, Education, and Welfare, Office of Education Bulletin 1961, No. 3. Washington, D.C.: U.S. Government Printing Office, 1961.

Falvey, Frances E., *Student Participation in College Administration.* New York: Bureau of Publications, Teachers College, 1952.

Farnsworth, Dana L., *College Health Services in the United States.* Washington, D.C.: American College Personnel Association, 1965.

———, *Mental Health in College and University.* Cambridge: Harvard University Press, 1957.

Feder, Daniel D., *et al., The Administration of Student Personnel Programs in American Colleges and Universities, Council Studies,* Series VI, No. 19. Washington, D.C.: American Council on Education, 1958.

Frederick, Robert W., *Student Activities in American Education.* New York: The Center for Applied Research in Education, Inc., 1965.

Funkenstein, Daniel H., ed., *The Student and Mental Health: An International View*. Cambridge, Mass.: The Riverside Press, 1959.

Gibson, Raymond C., *The Challenge of Leadership in Higher Education*. Dubuque, Ia.: William C. Brown Co., Publishers, 1964.

Hahn, Milton E., and Malcolm S. MacLean, *Counseling Psychology*. New York: McGraw-Hill Book Company, 1955.

Kemp, Gratton, *Perspectives on the Group Process*. Boston: Houghton Mifflin, 1964.

Kerr, Clark, *The Uses of the University*. Cambridge, Mass.: Harvard University Press, 1963.

Klopf, Gordon, *College Student Government*. New York: Harper and Brothers, 1960.

Leonard, Eugenie A., *Origins of Personnel Services in American Higher Education*. Minneapolis, Minn.: University of Minnesota Press, 1956.

Lundsford, Terry F., ed., *The Study of Campus Cultures*. Boulder, Colo.: Western Interstate Commission for Higher Education, 1963.

Lunn, Harry H., ed., *The Student's Role in College Policy Making*. Washington, D.C.: American Council on Education, 1957.

McGowan, John F., and Lyle D. Schmidt, *Counseling: Readings in Theory and Practice*. New York: Holt, Rinehart and Winston, Inc., 1962.

Millett, John D., *The Academic Community: An Essay on Organization*. New York: McGraw-Hill Book Company, 1962.

Mueller, Kate Hevner, *Student Personnel Work in Higher Education*. Boston: Houghton Mifflin, 1961.

Riker, Harold C., *College Housing as Learning Centers*. Washington, D.C.: American Personnel and Guidance Association, 1965.

———, *College Students Live Here*. New York: Educational Facilities Laboratory, 1961.

———, *Planning Functional College Housing*. New York: Teachers College, Columbia University, 1956.

Sanford, Nevitt, ed., *The American College: A Psychological and Social Interpretation of the Higher Learning*. New York: John Wiley & Sons, Inc., 1962.

Scott, William A., *Values and Organizations: A Study of Fraternities and Sororities*. Chicago: Rand McNally & Co., 1965.

Sprague, Hall T., ed., *Research on College Students*. Boulder, Colo.: Western Interstate Commission for Higher Education, 1960.

Steffire, Buford, *Theories of Counseling*. New York: McGraw-Hill Book Company, 1965.

Stroup, Herbert, *Toward a Philosophy of Organized Student Activities*. Minneapolis, Minn.: University of Minnesota Press, 1964.

Tyler, Leona E., *The Work of the Counselor*. New York: Appleton-Century-Crofts, 1961.

West, Elmer D., *Financial Aid to the Undergraduate—Issues and Implications*. Washington, D.C.: American Council on Education, 1963.

Williamson, E. G., *Student Personnel Services in Colleges and Universities.* New York: McGraw-Hill Book Company, 1961.

Wise, W. Max, *They Come for the Best of Reasons: College Students Today.* Washington, D.C.: American Council on Education, 1958.

Wrenn, C. Gilbert, *Student Personnel Work in Colleges.* New York: Ronald Press, 1951.

Index